CSET®

Foundational-Level General Science Practice Questions

Mometrix
TEST PREPARATION

DEAR FUTURE EXAM SUCCESS STORY

First of all, **THANK YOU** for purchasing Mometrix study materials!

Second, congratulations! You are one of the few determined test-takers who are committed to doing whatever it takes to excel on your exam. **You have come to the right place.** We developed these practice tests with one goal in mind: to deliver you the best possible approximation of the questions you will see on test day.

Standardized testing is one of the biggest obstacles on your road to success, which only increases the importance of doing well in the high-pressure, high-stakes environment of test day. Your results on this test could have a significant impact on your future, and these practice tests will give you the repetitions you need to build your familiarity and confidence with the test content and format to help you achieve your full potential on test day.

Your success is our success

We would love to hear from you! If you would like to share the story of your exam success or if you have any questions or comments in regard to our products, please contact us at **800-673-8175** or **support@mometrix.com**.

Thanks again for your business and we wish you continued success!

Sincerely,
The Mometrix Test Preparation Team

TABLE OF CONTENTS

Practice Test #1

1. Which of the following is the smallest?

a. Tissue
b. Cell
c. Muscle
d. Ligament

2. Which of the following statements correctly describes an effect of the Gulf Stream?

a. It increases humidity along North America's west coast.
b. It makes the climate of South America colder.
c. It makes the climate of Northern Europe warmer.
d. It makes the climate of the Caribbean milder and less humid.

3. According to Coulomb's law of electric force, which of the following statements is true?

a. The force between two charged objects is directly proportional to the square of the distance between them.
b. The force between two charged objects is inversely related to the square of the distance between them.
c. The force between two charged objects is inversely related to the distance between them.
d. The force between two charged objects is inversely related to the square root of the distance between them.

4. Which of the following statements regarding the principle of uniformitarianism is true?

a. Uniformitarianism is an argument for catastrophism.
b. Uniformitarianism is a key building block for Darwin's theory of evolution.
c. Uniformitarianism states that the past is the key to the present.
d. Uniformitarianism states that the fittest organisms will survive to reproduce.

5. The specific heat capacity of ice is half as much as that of liquid water. What is the result of this?

a. It takes half the amount of energy to increase the temperature of a 1 kg sample of ice by 1 °C than a 1 kg sample of water.
b. It takes twice the amount of energy to increase the temperature of a 1 kg sample of ice by 1 °C than a 1 kg sample of water.
c. It takes a quarter the amount of energy to increase the temperature of a 1 kg sample of ice by 1 °C than a 1 kg sample of water.
d. It takes the same amount of energy to increase the temperature of a 1 kg sample of ice and a 1 kg sample of water by 1 °C.

6. Which of the following statements correctly compares rocks and minerals?

a. Minerals may contain traces of organic compounds, while rocks do not.
b. Rocks are classified by their formation and the minerals they contain, while minerals are classified by their chemical composition and physical properties.
c. Both rocks and minerals can be polymorphs.
d. Both rocks and minerals may contain mineraloids.

7. Which of the following is a disadvantage of biomass energy?

a. Using it releases a lot of carbon.
b. It is non-renewable.
c. It requires a lot of space.
d. Current processes require rare earth metals to utilize the energy.

8. When materials that are attracted by magnets align at right angles to the lines of the magnetic force field, the name for this is:

a. Magnetic induction
b. Ferromagnetism
c. Paramagnetism
d. Diamagnetism

9. When a population reaches its carrying capacity:

a. Other populations will be forced out of the habitat.
b. Density-dependent factors no longer play a role.
c. Density-independent factors no longer play a role.
d. The population growth rate approaches zero.

10. Which of the following best describes the primary function of carbohydrates?

a. Provide energy
b. Aid in metabolism
c. Muscle tissue function
d. Prevents cell damage

11. Water is likely to have the shortest residence time in which of the following types of reservoirs?

a. A glacier
b. A lake
c. A river
d. The atmosphere

12. A tropical flower is planted in a local garden. The garden is watered 2 to 3 times per week during all seasons. After only a few months, the tropical plant begins to droop and turn brown. How did environmental change most likely affect the tropical plant?

a. Being watered 2 to 3 times per week was not enough to sustain a tropical plant.
b. The new environment was too hot and burned the plant.
c. Insects attacked the plant causing it to wilt.
d. The new soil lacked the nutrients necessary to maintain the plant's health.

13. Which of the following is the mathematical principle used to calculate a user's position based on information from the GPS satellites in the user's area?

a. Triangulation
b. Trilateration
c. Quadlateration
d. Quadangulation

14. Which of the following measurements is equal to 25.4 centimeters?

a. 10 in
b. 2.1 ft
c. 2.54 m
d. 2,540 mm

Refer to the following for question 15:

> Your 9th grade biology class is about to take on its first animal dissection. You have already covered the procedure in detail during class, but you know that some of the students are still feeling nervous or even a little queasy.

15. Which of the following procedures would be INCORRECT regarding dissection?

a. The specimen should be rinsed before handling.
b. Harmful chemicals should be disposed of according to district regulations.
c. Decaying specimens are never permitted.
d. Students with open sores on their hands that cannot be covered should be excused from the dissection.

16. What is a potential drawback that medical advances could have for human life?

a. Medical advances require humans to constantly re-examine their moral beliefs.
b. Medical advances have drastically increased the human life span, placing stress on the environment and the economy.
c. While medical advances have cured many diseases, new diseases may still arise and threaten lives.
d. Medical advances have given people many more opportunities for treatments and drugs depending on what they can afford.

17. Which of the following is NOT an example of chemical weathering of rocks?

a. Highly acidic rainwater causes dissolution of rocks.
b. Anhydrous minerals in rocks absorb water, causing them to enlarge and create fractures within the rocks.
c. Salt water penetrates fractures in rocks and leaves behind salt crystals that cause fractures.
d. Iron atoms in rocks react with atmospheric oxygen, which causes oxidation.

18. All of the following are true regarding wind energy, EXCEPT:

a. Wind turbines use space inefficiently, but they have low operational costs.
b. Wind is not a reliable source of energy in all geographic locations.
c. Wind turbines are expensive to manufacture and install.
d. Wind turbines are a threat to wildlife.

19. Which of the following is considered observational evidence in support of the Big Bang Theory?

a. Expansion in the redshifts of galaxies
b. Measurements of cosmic microwave background radiation
c. Measurements of the distribution of quasars and galaxies
d. All of the above

20. A weather balloon is filled with 1,000 mol of He gas at 25 °C and 101 kPa of pressure. What is the volume of the weather balloon?

a. 24,518 m^3
b. 24.5 m^3
c. 2 m^3
d. 245 m^3

21. A space station is revolving in a circular orbit around Earth. Consider the following three statements:

I. The center of mass of the space station is necessarily located at its geometric center.
II. The center of mass is moving at a constant velocity.
III. The center of mass of the space station is moving at a constant speed.

Which of the following statements is true?

a. I is true.
b. II is true.
c. III is true.
d. I, II, and III are not true.

22. According to the kinetic theory of matter, which of the following statements is true?

a. The average kinetic energy is inversely proportional to the square of the average velocity of the particles.
b. The average kinetic energy is inversely proportional to the average velocity of the particles.
c. The average kinetic energy is directly proportional to the square of the average velocity of the particles.
d. The average kinetic energy is directly proportional to the average velocity of the particles.

23. Which type of nuclear process features atomic nuclei splitting apart to form smaller nuclei?

a. Fission
b. Fusion
c. Decay
d. Ionization

24. A worker applies a force of 500.0 N to a pulley for a distance of 1.5 m to move a crate that weighs 1,000.0 N a distance of 0.5 m. What is the ideal mechanical advantage of this pulley?

a. 4
b. 2
c. 3
d. 5

25. You are watching the Olympic ice skating championships and see the pairs are up next. They begin their routine facing each other with their palms up and against each other. When the music starts, they push themselves apart with their palms. What type of force is this?

a. Magnetic
b. Balanced
c. Action and reaction force
d. Centripetal force

Refer to the following for question 26:

After a laboratory experiment that involved using various chemical solutions, you and your lab partner are asked to clean up your workspace. The teacher states that any chemicals that have been poured into a new container should be disposed of, but the chemicals still in their original bottles can be placed into storage.

26. Which of the following is NOT a recommended storage practice for laboratory chemicals?

a. Chemicals should be stored at the appropriate temperature and humidity.
b. Chemicals should be dated when received and when opened.
c. Chemicals may be routinely stored on bench tops.
d. Chemicals should be stored on shelves with raised outer edges.

27. Consider the two vectors below:

Vector A:
Vector B:

Which vector best represents the vector obtained by subtracting *A* from *B* $(\vec{B} - \vec{A})$?

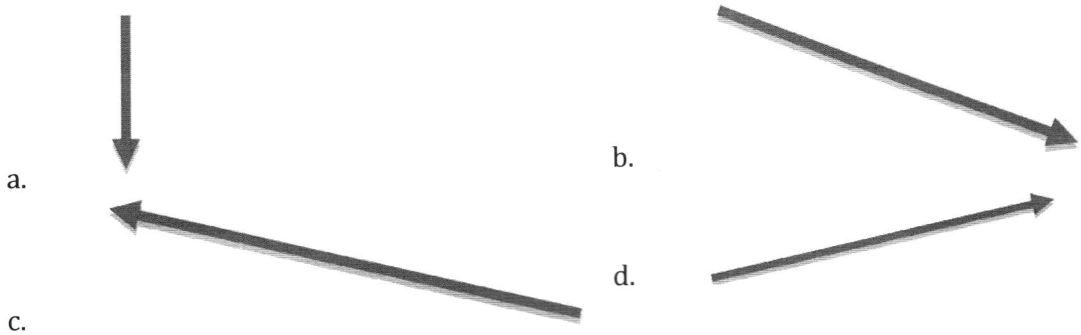

28. Metamorphic rock is produced when which of the following undergoes profound changes as a result of exposure to intense pressure and heat?

a. A batholith
b. A protolith
c. An igneous rock
d. A sedimentary rock

Refer to the following for question 29:

1 IA	2 IIA	3 IIIB	4 IVB	5 VB	6 VIB	7 VIIB	8	9 VIIIB	10	11 IB	12 IIB	13 IIIA	14 IVA	15 VA	16 VIA	17 VIIA	18 VIIIA
1 **H** 1.01																	2 **He** 4.00
3 **Li** 6.94	4 **Be** 9.01											5 **B** 10.81	6 **C** 12.01	7 **N** 14.01	8 **O** 16.00	9 **F** 19.00	10 **Ne** 20.18
11 **Na** 22.99	12 **Mg** 24.31											13 **Al** 26.98	14 **Si** 28.09	15 **P** 30.97	16 **S** 32.07	17 **Cl** 35.45	18 **Ar** 39.95
19 **K** 39.1	20 **Ca** 40.08	21 **Sc** 44.96	22 **Ti** 47.88	23 **V** 50.94	24 **Cr** 52.00	25 **Mn** 54.94	26 **Fe** 55.85	27 **Co** 58.93	28 **Ni** 58.69	29 **Cu** 63.55	30 **Zn** 65.39	31 **Ga** 69.72	32 **Ge** 72.61	33 **As** 74.92	34 **Se** 78.96	35 **Br** 79.90	36 **Kr** 83.80
37 **Rb** 85.47	38 **Sr** 87.62	39 **Y** 88.91	40 **Zr** 91.22	41 **Nb** 92.91	42 **Mo** 95.94	43 **Tc** (98)	44 **Ru** 101.07	45 **Rh** 102.91	46 **Pd** 106.42	47 **Ag** 107.87	48 **Cd** 112.41	49 **In** 114.82	50 **Sn** 118.71	51 **Sb** 121.76	52 **Te** 127.6	53 **I** 126.9	54 **Xe** 131.29
55 **Cs** 132.9	56 **Ba** 137.3	57 **La*** 138.9	72 **Hf** 178.5	73 **Ta** 180.9	74 **W** 183.9	75 **Re** 186.2	76 **Os** 190.2	77 **Ir** 192.2	78 **Pt** 195.1	79 **Au** 197.0	80 **Hg** 200.6	81 **Tl** 204.4	82 **Pb** 207.2	83 **Bi** 209	84 **Po** (209)	85 **At** (210)	86 **Rn** (222)
87 **Fr** (223)	88 **Ra** (226)	89 **Ac^** (227)	104 **Rf** (261)	105 **Db** (262)	106 **Sg** (263)	107 **Bh** (264)	108 **Hs** (265)	109 **Mt** (268)	110 **Ds** (271)	111 **Rg** (272)							

*	58 **Ce** 140.1	59 **Pr** 140.9	60 **Nd** 144.2	61 **Pm** (145)	62 **Sm** 150.4	63 **Eu** 152.0	64 **Gd** 157.3	65 **Tb** 158.9	66 **Dy** 162.5	67 **Ho** 164.9	68 **Er** 167.3	69 **Tm** 168.9	70 **Yb** 173.0	71 **Lu** 175.0
^	90 **Th** 232.0	91 **Pa** (231)	92 **U** 238.0	93 **Np** (237)	94 **Pu** (244)	95 **Am** (243)	96 **Cm** (247)	97 **Bk** (247)	98 **Cf** (251)	99 **Es** (252)	100 **Fm** (257)	101 **Md** (258)	102 **No** (259)	103 **Lr** (260)

*Note: The row labeled with * is the lanthanide series, and the row labeled with ^ is the actinide series.*

29. On average, how many neutrons does one atom of bromine (Br) have?

a. 35
b. 44.9
c. 45
d. 79.9

30. Which of the following statements is NOT congruent with the theory of plate tectonics?

a. The continents were once connected in the large supercontinent Pangea.
b. The tectonic plates are part of the Earth's lithosphere.
c. Seafloor spreading is evidence of tectonic plate movement.
d. Subduction occurs at divergent boundaries.

31. Which of the following equations for sound waves correctly relates frequency to wavelength and speed of sound?

a. $f \times \lambda = v$
b. $f = \lambda \times v$
c. $f = \lambda + v$
d. $f \times \lambda \times v = 1$

32. Which of the following types of rock solidifies deepest beneath the Earth's surface?

a. Hypabyssal
b. Plutonic
c. Volcanic
d. Detrital

33. Which of the following has the potential for negative impacts including soil contamination, surface water contamination, pollution, and leachate?

a. Landfills
b. Incinerators
c. Recycling centers
d. Irrigation systems

34. Which of the following statements regarding the layers of the atmosphere is NOT true?

a. In the troposphere, temperature decreases as altitude increases.
b. In the mesosphere, temperature decreases as altitude increases.
c. In the stratosphere, temperature decreases as altitude increases.
d. In the thermosphere, temperature increases as altitude increases.

35. Minerals that form on the sea floor from discarded shells are most likely part of which chemical class?

a. Sulfate
b. Organic
c. Carbonate
d. Silicate

36. Which of the following lists some of the vertebrae in the human skeleton in descending order?

a. Atlas, axis, thoracic, lumbar, sacral, coccyx
b. Axis, sacral, coccyx, atlas, lumbar, thoracic
c. Thoracic, sacral, lumbar, axis, coccyx, atlas
d. Coccyx, lumbar, axis, sacral, thoracic, atlas

37. This organelle contains digestive enzymes that break down food and unneeded substances. They are also thought to be linked to the aging process. What part of a cell does this describe?

a. Lysosomes
b. Chromatin
c. Plastids
d. Golgi apparatus

38. What is an assumed explanation for an occurrence that is based on prior knowledge called?

a. Independent variable
b. Dependent variable
c. Trial
d. Hypothesis

39. Under which conditions will light undergo total internal reflection?

a. When the angle of incidence is equal to the critical angle
b. When the angle of incidence is greater than the critical angle
c. When the angle of incidence is less than the critical angle
d. When the angle of incidence is zero

40. Which combination of household chemicals produces a toxic gas?

a. Baking soda and vinegar
b. Bleach and ammonia
c. Water and sugar
d. Vinegar and antacid tablets
e. Rubbing alcohol and table salt

41. The year-round warmth of tropical rainforests is best explained by:

a. Their proximity to warm ocean currents
b. The forest canopy's ability to trap heat
c. The high humidity caused by frequent rainfall
d. Regular, intense solar energy

42. Suppose your actual weight is 150 pounds and you weigh yourself with an analog scale and get a reading of 152.1 pounds. You repeat the measurement twice more and get 152.1 pounds each time. Which of the following statements is true?

a. There is no random error.
b. There is no systematic error.
c. The systematic error is 2.1 pounds.
d. The random error is 2.1 pounds.

43. Which of the following is a risk in the genetic engineering of human beings?

a. Increasing diseases
b. Limiting our genetic diversity
c. Decreasing our life span
d. Eliminating birth defects

44. Which part of a hurricane features the strongest winds and greatest rainfall?

a. Eye wall
b. Front
c. Eye
d. Outward spiral

45. Evidence that humans share a common ancestor with other primates includes all of the following EXCEPT:

a. DNA sequence
b. Fossil evidence of intermediate species
c. Analogous structures
d. Homologous structures

46. Which of the following characteristics is consistent with an acid?

a. Turns litmus paper blue
b. Accepts a proton
c. Reacts with zinc to produce hydrogen gas
d. Produces OH^- ions in aqueous solutions

47. Which of the following is required for the activity of DNA polymerase?

a. Okazaki fragments
b. RNA primer
c. Single-strand binding protein
d. Leading strand

Refer to the following for question 48:

A sixth-grade science teacher tells her students that they will have a seismologist studying plate tectonics come to class. She has a group of early-intermediate English learners in her class. The seismologist will discuss what causes earthquakes, the effects of earthquakes, and any questions students might have on the topic.

48. One student wants to know what causes the shaking that occurs with an earthquake. What answer would the seismologist likely give to that student?

a. Static deformation
b. Seismic waves
c. Compression waves
d. Continental drift

49. When working in the laboratory, what is the minimum length of time an eye should be flushed if a chemical gets in the eye?

a. 2 minutes
b. 10 minutes
c. 15 minutes
d. 30 minutes

50. DNA electrophoresis accomplishes which of the following?

a. Breaking DNA into fragments
b. Separating DNA fragments by size
c. Extracting DNA from evidence
d. Identifying key genetic codes with radioactive markers

51. Which of the following is needed for an experiment to be considered successful?

a. A reasonable hypothesis
b. A well-written lab report
c. Data that others can reproduce
d. Computer-aided statistical analysis

52. What steps should precede drawing a conclusion about a hypothesis?

a. Testing, observing, and recording data
b. Communicating the hypothesis to others
c. Comparing data with data of other groups
d. Reporting the results so they can be replicated

53. Which of the following is NOT a product of respiration?

a. Carbon dioxide
b. Water
c. Glucose
d. ATP

54. Which of the following describes the process skill of concluding?

a. Explaining or interpreting observations
b. Making a determination based on the results of a controlled experiment
c. Reading an instrument during an experiment
d. Listing similarities and differences between two objects

55. When you walk barefoot on a hot sidewalk, what process is primarily responsible for heat transfer from the sidewalk to your foot?

a. Conduction
b. Convection
c. Radiation
d. None of the above.

56. Which of the following is an example of a chemical change?

a. Salt dissolving in water
b. Water evaporating
c. Silver tarnishing
d. Dry ice sublimating

57. Which of the following of Lamarck's evolutionary ideas turned out to be true?

a. Natural selection
b. Organisms naturally transform into increasingly complex organisms
c. Inheritance of acquired characters
d. Body parts develop with increased usage and weaken with disuse

58. Lions live in savannah and grassland regions where there are tall, dry grasses. Lions must sneak up and stalk their prey. What is the most likely reason for a lion's sand colored coat?

a. It allows lions to hide within the grass.
b. The light color of their coat reflects heat from the Sun.
c. A lion's coloring helps it attract mates.
d. It allows them to run faster than their prey.

59. Which of the following demographic changes would lead to a population with an older age composition?

a. Increased birth rate
b. Environmental pollution
c. Increased availability of food
d. Medical advancements that increase life expectancy

60. Jim and John are working on their science fair project when they accidently break a beaker. What should the boys do?

a. Tell their teacher immediately
b. Clean up the broken glass themselves
c. Move away from the broken glass and continue working
d. Hide the broken glass so they don't get in trouble

61. Which of the following habitats would provide an opportunity for secondary succession?

a. A retreating glacier
b. Burned cropland
c. A newly formed volcanic island
d. A 500-year-old forest

62. How do animals of the phylum Mollusca respire?

a. Through gills
b. Through a trachea
c. Through book lungs
d. Through muscle contraction

Refer to the following for question 63:

> The planet's oceans are experiencing climate changes, pollution, and overfishing. In some areas, zones that would normally host abundant aquatic life are now considered "dead zones."

63. Which of the following causes of ocean destruction is not a result of human activity?

a. Diminishment of coral reefs
b. Destruction of food webs
c. Tectonic plate shift
d. Degradation or total loss of wetlands

64. Which of the following is NOT an example of an oxidation-reduction reaction?

a. A volcano eruption can be modeled using vinegar and baking soda.
b. Steel cans are electroplated with tin to produce grocery store food cans.
c. Blood catalyzes the decomposition of hydrogen peroxide on a cut.
d. Bread dough rises from the production of carbon dioxide gas by yeast.

65. The center of an atom is called the ____. It is composed of ____.

a. nucleus; protons and neutrons
b. nucleus; protons and electrons
c. electron cloud; electrons and protons
d. electron cloud; electrons and neutrons

66. Mrs. Jones's class conducted an experiment on the effects of sugar and artificial sweetener on the cookie recipe's overall color when baked. What would be the independent variable in the cookie experiment?

a. The students should use the same ingredients in both recipes, but bake the cookies with sugar at 450 degrees and those with artificial sweetener at 475 degrees. They should increase the baking time on the artificial sweetener cookies, since the package instructs them to do so
b. The students should use the same ingredients in both recipes, but increase the baking time on the artificial sweetener cookies, since the package instructs them to do so
c. The students should use the same ingredients, same baking temperatures, and same baking times for both recipes
d. The students should use the same ingredients and baking times in both recipes, but bake the cookies with sugar at 450 degrees and the artificial sweetener cookies at 475 degrees

67. Which of the following divisions of plants produces seeds for reproduction?

a. Anthophyta
b. Lycophyta
c. Sphenophyta
d. Pterophyta

68. Which of the following subskills best fits the process skill of observing?

a. Using the five senses to collect evidence and write descriptions
b. Grouping objects based on similarities, differences, and interrelationships
c. Explaining or interpreting collected evidence
d. Reporting to others what has been found by experimentation

69. The mountain below has the oldest rock in its core and the youngest rock in its outer layers. Which of the following terms best describes the mountain?

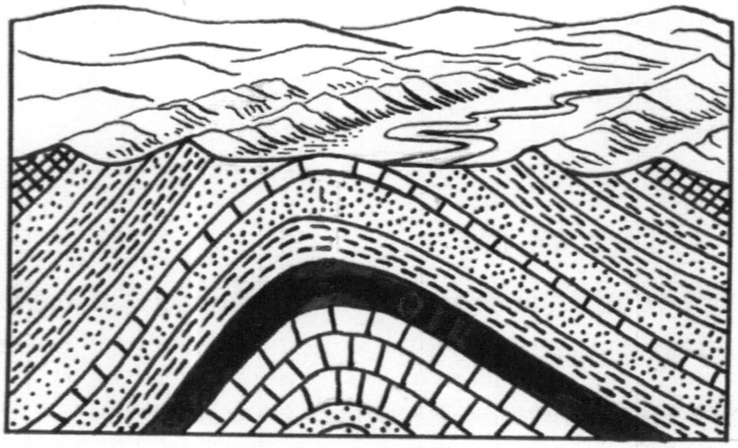

a. Syncline
b. Anticline
c. Fault-block
d. Graben

70. During a chemistry experiment, which of the data below would not be collected for your lab report?

a. Temperature changes
b. Color changes
c. Production of gas or odor
d. Observations of other trials

Refer to the following for question 71:

Let B represent the dominant allele for a full head of hair, and let b represent the recessive allele for male-pattern baldness. The following Punnett square represents the offspring of two people with recessive genes for baldness.

	B	**b**
B	Possibility 1	Possibility 2
b	Possibility 3	Possibility 4

71. According to the Punnett square, which possibility would produce an offspring with male-pattern baldness?

a. Possibility 1
b. Possibility 2
c. Possibility 3
d. Possibility 4

72. According to Ohm's Law, how are voltage and current related in an electrical circuit?

a. Voltage and current are inversely proportional to one another.
b. Voltage and current are directly proportional to one another.
c. Voltage acts to oppose the current along an electrical circuit.
d. Voltage acts to decrease the current along an electrical circuit.

73. Physical weathering of rocks can be caused by all of the following EXCEPT:

a. The freezing and thawing of water on the surface of rocks
b. Changes in temperature
c. Oxidation
d. Changes in pressure due to the removal of overlying rocks

74. What type of chemical bond connects the oxygen and hydrogen atoms in a molecule of water?

a. Static bond
b. Aquatic bond
c. Ionic bond
d. Covalent bond

75. Which of the following factors directly contributes to soil erosion?

a. Air pollution from cars and factories
b. Use of pesticides
c. Deforestation and overgrazing
d. Water pollution caused by excess sedimentation

76. Which of the following statements about galaxies is true?

a. Galaxies are the only structures in the universe that do not contain dark matter.
b. Galaxies are gravitationally bound, meaning structures within the galaxy orbit around its center.
c. Galaxies typically contain over one trillion stars.
d. Galaxies are composed of clusters and superclusters.

77. In the field of stratigraphy, the relative ages of rocks may be determined by examining which of the following types of evidence?

a. The dates the rocks were formed and the ages of fossils deposited within the rocks
b. Evidence of changes in detrital remanent magnetism when the rock was deposited
c. The vertical layering pattern of the rock
d. All of the above

Refer to the following for question 78:

A teacher in Arizona takes her class on a walk through a nearby park to study the flora and fauna of their local desert ecosystem. The students see cacti, snakes, and even evidence of coyote activity.

78. How should the teacher explain to students how these organisms are able to survive in harsh desert conditions?

a. Over thousands of years, these organisms have developed adaptations to survive in arid climates.
b. These organisms migrate out of the desert during the summer months, only living in the desert for a portion of the year.
c. Snakes, cacti, and coyotes work together to find sources of food and water.
d. Snakes, cacti, and coyotes are all aquatic species that live in ponds and rivers during the hot day.

79. After a science laboratory exercise, some solutions remain unused and are left over. What should be done with these solutions?

a. Dispose of the solutions according to local disposal procedures.
b. Empty the solutions into the sink and rinse with warm water and soap.
c. Ensure the solutions are secured in closed containers and throw away.
d. Store the solutions in a secured, dry place for later use.

80. How are lipids different from other organic molecules?

a. They consist of repeating monomers to form long chains.
b. They are not water soluble.
c. They serve as catalysts.
d. Lipids store less energy per gram than carbohydrates or proteins.

81. Which of the following correctly describes the impact science has had on HIV?

a. HIV has been eradicated by vaccinations of inactivated HIV.
b. The progression from HIV to AIDS can be controlled by antiretroviral drugs.
c. HIV can be cured by antiretroviral drugs.
d. HIV mutations have been prevented by antiretroviral drugs.

82. How does the loss of biodiversity directly impact the environment and society?

a. Increase of access to raw materials
b. Increase of access to clean water
c. Decrease of food supply
d. Decrease of vulnerability to natural disasters

83. When we look at a straw in a glass of water, the straw appears broken or bent at the waterline. This appearance is a function of:

a. Scattering
b. Absorption
c. Reflection
d. Refraction

84. Which of the following is NOT true concerning forming and testing hypotheses?

a. A controlled experiment should have only one independent variable.
b. A controlled experiment may have several constants.
c. A good hypothesis should take all of the available background material on the topic into consideration.
d. A good hypothesis will not be disproved by testing.

85. A teacher tells the class about a new drug that is being tested on 200 volunteer subjects. Half the volunteers are given the new drug while the other half are given a harmless sugar pill. The volunteers who are given the sugar pill serve as the:

a. Control group
b. Experimental group
c. Variable
d. Indicator

86. Which of the following describes the correct short-term storage method for liquid-filled pH probes?

a. Store the pH probes in distilled water.
b. Store the pH probes on a dry shelf.
c. Store the pH probes in a potassium chloride solution.
d. Store the pH probes in hydrochloric acid.

Refer to the following for question 87:

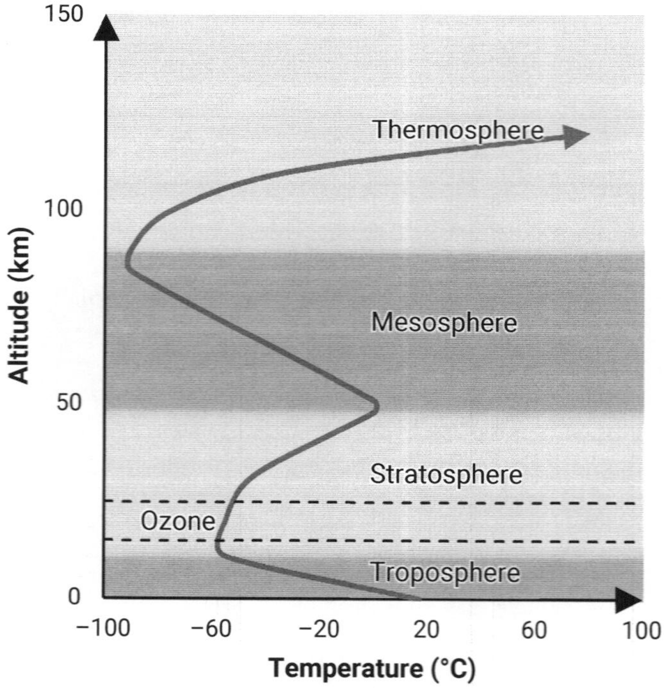

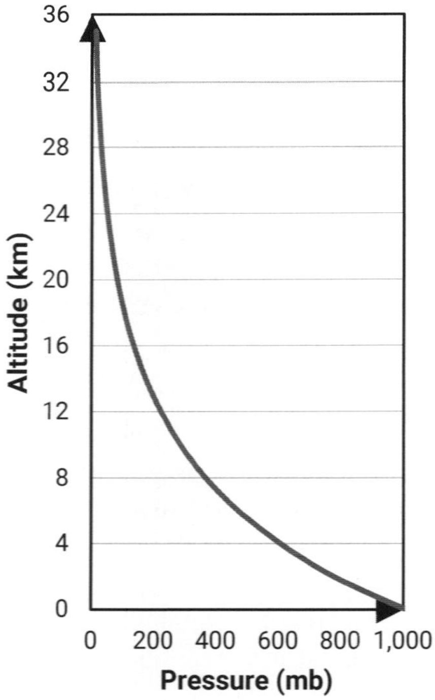

The Earth's atmosphere is comprised of multiple layers with very different temperature characteristics. Closest to the surface, the *troposphere* contains approximately 75 percent of the atmosphere's mass and 99 percent of its water vapor and aerosols. Temperature fluctuations cause constant mixing of air in the troposphere through convection, but it generally becomes cooler as altitude increases.

The *stratosphere* is heated by the absorption of ultraviolet radiation from the sun. Since its lower layers are composed of cooler, heavier air, there is no convective mixing in the stratosphere, and it is quite stable.

The *mesosphere* is the atmospheric layer directly above the stratosphere. Here, temperature decreases as altitude increases due to decreased solar heating and—to a degree—CO_2. In the lower atmosphere, CO_2 acts as a greenhouse gas by absorbing infrared radiation from the Earth's surface. In the mesosphere, CO_2 cools the atmosphere by radiating heat into space.

Above this layer lies the *thermosphere*. At these altitudes, atmospheric gases form layers according to their molecular masses. Temperatures increase with altitude due to absorption of solar radiation by the small amount of residual oxygen. Temperatures are highly dependent on solar activity and can rise to 1,500 °C.

87. The lowest temperatures in the Earth's atmosphere are recorded within the:

a. Troposphere
b. Stratosphere
c. Mesosphere
d. Thermosphere

88. A leading drug company has created a drug that can help cure diabetes, but before it can go on the market, the company must first prove that it works. The scientists use the drug on a group of 100 people and provide a placebo to another 100 people; neither group knows if they have received the drug or the placebo. All other factors, such as exercise, diet, and amount of sleep, have stayed the same. What is this experiment using to determine if the drug works?

a. A standard deviation
b. A dependent variable
c. A hypothesis
d. A control group

89. The distance from the earth to the sun is equal to which of the following?

a. One astronomical unit
b. One light-year
c. One parsec
d. One arcsecond

90. All of the following are common ways of controlling eukaryotic gene expression EXCEPT:

a. Regulatory proteins
b. Nucleosome packing
c. Methylation of DNA
d. Operons

91. Which of the following creates a magnetic field?

a. The spinning and rotating of electrons in atoms
b. The separation of charged particles in atoms
c. The vibrational and translational motion of atoms
d. Loosely held valence electrons surrounding an atom

92. Which of the following common household products is NOT correctly matched with the chemical associated with it?

a. Vinegar and acetic acid
b. Glass cleaner and sodium hypochlorite
c. Baking soda and sodium bicarbonate
d. Rubbing alcohol and isopropanol

93. Rocks are classified as *igneous*, *metamorphic*, or *sedimentary* based on:

a. How they were formed
b. Their texture
c. The minerals they contain
d. Their age

94. A prairie ecosystem is described below. Farmers treat fields surrounding the prairie with pesticides that kill part of the beetle population. What effect would the pesticides have on the rest of the ecosystem?

Grass is eaten by grasshoppers, rabbits, and crickets
Corn is eaten by squirrels and beetles
Grasshoppers, beetles, and crickets are all eaten by birds
Squirrels, birds, and rabbits are all eaten by both foxes and coyotes

a. There would be a decrease in the cricket population.
b. There would be an increase in the population of birds.
c. The population of rabbits would decrease.
d. The population of foxes would increase.

95. Which of the following is NOT a result of ozone layer depletion?

a. Higher UV levels reaching the Earth
b. Increased vitamin D synthesis
c. Damage to marine life such as plankton
d. Increased crop yields of wheat, corn, and soybeans

96. Heat is transmitted through solid materials via:

a. Conduction
b. Convection
c. Radiation
d. All three

97. The most severe mass extinction event in Earth's history was the:

a. Cretaceous-Tertiary Event
b. Permian-Triassic Event
c. Ordovician-Silurian Event
d. Late Devonian Event

98. Which of the following is considered a non-renewable resource?

a. Glass
b. Wood
c. Cattle
d. Soil

99. In humans, more than one gene contributes to the trait of hair color. What is this an example of

a. Pleiotropy
b. Polygenic inheritance
c. Codominance
d. Linkage

100. Which of the following statements is NOT true?

a. The Earth rotates on its axis once every 24 hours.
b. A solar eclipse can only occur during a new moon.
c. The Moon rotates on its axis as it revolves around the Earth.
d. A lunar eclipse occurs when the Moon passes between the Earth and the Sun.

Answer Key and Explanations for Test #1

1. B: Collections of cells form tissues (A), and collections of tissues can form muscles (C), making cells the smallest of the three. A ligament (D) is a band of dense connective tissue that connects bones, meaning that it is composed of many cells and is therefore larger than a single cell.

2. C: The Gulf Stream, which is a surface current that originates in the Gulf of Mexico and travels across the Atlantic Ocean, makes the climate of Northern Europe warmer. After traveling up the eastern coast of the US, the Gulf Stream splits into two forks. The North Atlantic Drift travels across the ocean to warm Europe, while the southern fork travels toward West Africa.

3. B: Coulomb's law of electric force is represented by $F = k\frac{q_1 q_2}{d^2}$ in which F is the electrostatic force, k is a constant related to the medium between the charges, q_1 and q_2 are the strengths of the charges, and d is the distance between the charges. Since the square of the distance is in the denominator, the force is inversely related to the square of the distance between the charges.

4. B: Darwin studied Lyell's work *Principles of Geology* while sailing around South America and the Galapagos Islands. Lyell's theory of uniformitarianism supposes that all things are continuing in the same uniform natural processes and that the changes to the Earth's crust have arisen from these continuous, uniform processes. Darwin was inspired by this theory and used it as a foundation for his theory of evolution, adopting the phrase that "the present is the key to the past" to the evolutionary history of life on Earth. Choice C is incorrect because it reverses the phrase. Choice A is incorrect because uniformitarianism is completely opposed to the idea of catastrophism, which argues that the majority of Earth's features are a result of violent, sudden events, such as meteorites and other natural disasters. Finally, D is incorrect because natural selection states that the fittest organisms will survive to reproduce.

5. A: Heat capacity refers to the amount of heat or thermal energy required to raise the temperature of a specific substance by a given unit. A substance with a higher heat capacity requires more heat to raise its temperature than a substance with a lower heat capacity. The comparison here is that the specific heat capacity of ice is half as much as that of liquid water, so it takes half the amount of energy to increase the same amount of ice one temperature unit than it would if it were liquid water.

6. B: It is true that rocks are classified by their formation and the minerals they contain, while minerals are classified by their chemical composition and physical properties. Choice A is incorrect because rocks may contain traces of organic compounds. Choices C and D are incorrect because only minerals can be polymorphs and only rocks contain mineraloids.

7. C: Advantages of biomass energy include that it's renewable, carbon neutral, and abundant. A disadvantage of biomass energy include that it requires space and may be inefficient.

8. D: Diamagnetic materials align perpendicularly to magnetic field lines, and do not retain magnetic properties when the external magnetic field is removed. These include copper, silver, gold, and most other elements in the periodic table. Paramagnetic (C) materials align parallel to magnetic field lines, and also do not retain magnetic properties upon removal of the external field. These include lithium, magnesium, molybdenum, and tantalum. Ferromagnetic (B) materials retain their magnetic properties even when the external magnetic field is removed. These include iron, nickel, and cobalt. Magnetic induction (A) is the name for the process whereby magnets turn magnetic substances near them into magnets as well.

9. D: Within a habitat, there is a maximum number of individuals that can continue to thrive, known as the habitat's carrying capacity. When the population size approaches this number, population growth will stop.

10. A: Carbohydrates are the primary source of energy for the body. Proteins and lipids also provide energy, but are not as readily digestible to use actively. The Dietary Guidelines for Americans recommend that 45-65% of food intake consist of carbohydrates. Vitamins and minerals aid in metabolism and allow for cellular repair. Fats and proteins are available for energy if the body needs them, but the primary function of fats is to support cell growth and regulation of bodily functions, while the primary function of proteins is to help repair and build muscle tissue and to regulate chemical balances in the body.

11. D: Water is likely to have the shortest residence time in the atmosphere. Water molecules linger in the atmosphere for an estimated 9 days, while their residence time in glaciers may range from 20 to 100 years. Water molecules reside in lakes for approximately 50 to 100 years, and they stay in rivers for two to six months.

12. A: Tropical environments typically receive rain 5 to 6 times per week, even if it is only a brief afternoon shower. In its new environment, the tropical plant is not receiving enough water to survive.

13. B: A communication GPS receiver uses trilateration by timing signals from at least four satellites in the Global Positioning System. This allows it to determine its 3D position (latitude, longitude, and altitude) while also correcting for the receiver's clock error. Trilateration determines position, speed, and elevation. Trilateration differs from triangulation in that trilateration calculations use distances, while triangulation calculations use angles.

14. A: The conversion is done as follows: $(25.4 \text{ cm}) \times \left(\frac{1 \text{ in}}{2.54 \text{ cm}}\right) = 10 \text{ in}$. Choice B is arrived at by using the following incorrect formula: $(25.4 \text{ cm}) \times \left(\frac{1 \text{ ft}}{12 \text{ cm}}\right)$. Choice C is arrived at by using the following incorrect formula: $(25.4 \text{ cm}) \times \left(\frac{1 \text{ m}}{10 \text{ cm}}\right)$. Converting from centimeters to meters requires the use of the following formula: $(\text{cm}) \times \left(\frac{1 \text{ m}}{100 \text{ cm}}\right)$. Choice D is arrived at by using the following incorrect formula: $(25.4 \text{ cm}) \times \left(\frac{100 \text{ mm}}{1 \text{ cm}}\right)$. Converting from centimeters to millimeters requires the use of the following formula: $(\text{cm}) \times \left(\frac{10 \text{ mm}}{1 \text{ cm}}\right)$.

15. C: When performing a dissection in class, decaying specimens can be permitted under certain circumstances, but unknown specimens are never permitted. Rinsing the specimen before handling can help wash away excess preservative, which may be irritating. Disposing of harmful chemicals according to district regulations is always required. Excusing students with open sores on their hands that cannot be covered is a good precaution. Exposure to pathogens and toxic chemicals can occur through open breaks in the skin.

16. B: A longer life span does not necessarily lead to more productive years. It also leads to a larger aged population and increases the rate of population growth. Re-examining moral beliefs is not necessarily a drawback. New diseases may arise but medical advances may aid in the cure of these diseases.

17. C: When salt water penetrates fractures in rocks and leaves behind salt crystals that cause the rock to fracture, it is considered physical rather than chemical weathering. Chemical weathering involves changes in the molecules that make up the rocks, while physical weathering occurs when external factors act on the rock without changing its chemical composition in any way.

18. A: Pros of wind energy include space efficiency, no pollution, and low operational costs. Cons of wind energy include wind fluctuation, threats to wildlife, and the expense to manufacture and install.

19. D: Expansion in the redshifts of galaxies, measurements of cosmic microwave background radiation, and measurements of the distribution of quasars and galaxies are all considered observational evidence in support of the Big Bang Theory. The abundance of certain "primordial elements" is also consistent with the theory.

20. B: The ideal gas law $PV = nRT$ is rearranged to solve for V, and we get $V = \frac{nRT}{P}$. R is the gas constant, $\frac{0.08206 \text{ L atm}}{\text{mol K}}$, and the Celsius temperature must be converted to Kelvin, by adding 273 to 25 °C to obtain 298 K. The pressure must be converted to atmospheres, which 101 kPa is essentially 1 atm (0.9967 atm). Plugging the numbers into the equation, we get $V = 1{,}000 \text{ mol} \times \frac{\left(\frac{0.08206 \text{ L atm}}{\text{mol K}}\right)(298 \text{ K})}{1 \text{ atm}}$, which gives $V = 24{,}453$ L. A liter is a cubic decimeter (dm^3), and when converted, this gives $V = 24.5 \text{ m}^3$.

21. C: In a uniform gravitational field, such as occurs near Earth's surface, an object will move like a point mass located at the center of mass. However, this does not necessarily mean that the geometrical center of an object is the same as its center of mass, depending on its shape, design and mass distribution. The center of mass of a sphere or cube is at its geometric center because you can imagine the sphere as consisting of a large number of point masses located at certain points in space. Multiplying the point masses by their location and dividing by the total mass gives the center of mass. Statement I is not true because the space station may not be completely symmetrical. Statement III is true because the space station is undergoing uniform circular motion around Earth. If the orbit had been elliptical, this would not be true because the speed would have changed depending on the station's position. However, even though the speed is constant in a circular orbit, the velocity is not. Since velocity has a direction associated with it, and the space station is moving in a circular path, its velocity is constantly changing.

22. C: According to the kinetic theory of matter, the kinetic energy of a particle is found by $KE = \frac{1}{2}mv^2$ in which KE is the kinetic energy in Joules, m is the mass of the particle in kilograms, and v is the velocity of the particle in meters per second. This formula shows that the average kinetic energy is directly proportional to the square of the average velocity of the particles.

23. A: Fission is a nuclear process where atomic nuclei split apart to form smaller nuclei. Nuclear fission can release large amounts of energy, emit gamma rays, and form daughter products. It is used in nuclear power plants and bombs. Choice B, fusion, refers to a nuclear process whereby atomic nuclei join to form a heavier nucleus, such as with stars. This can release or absorb energy depending upon the original elements. Choice C, decay, refers to an atomic nucleus spontaneously losing energy and emitting ionizing particles and radiation. Choice D, ionization, refers to a process by which atoms obtain a positive or negative charge because the number of electrons does not equal that of protons.

24. C: The ideal mechanical advantage of a simple machine is determined by the ratio of input distance to output distance. Since the input distance is 1.5 m and the output distance is 0.5 m, the ideal mechanical advantage for this pulley is 3.

25. C: The ice skaters are applying Newton's Third Law to create an equal and opposite reaction force, causing both partners to move. When one skater pushes on the other, the other pushes back with equal and opposite force.

26. C: Chemicals should not be stored routinely on bench tops. Each chemical should be stored in a location for that specific type of chemical. When in use, chemicals may be temporarily kept on bench tops, but only in the quantities that are required for that particular situation. Chemicals should be returned to an appropriate location after use.

27. C: To add and subtract vectors algebraically, you add and subtract their components. To add vectors graphically, you shift the location of the vectors so that they are connected tip-to-tail. The resultant is a vector that starts at the tail of the first vector and ends at the tip of the second. To subtract vectors, connect the vectors tip to tail, starting with the vector that is not subtracted, and ending with the one that is. Think of this just like vector addition, except the vector that is subtracted (the one with the negative sign in front of it) switches directions.

28. B: Metamorphic rock is produced when a protolith undergoes profound changes after being exposed to extreme heat and pressure. A protolith is any rock that is transformed through this process. The original rock may be sedimentary, igneous, or metamorphic. The extreme heat and pressure that serve as the catalyst for this transformation may be produced by the intrusion of magma or tectonic activity, among other factors.

29. B: To determine the average number of neutrons in one atom of an element, subtract the atomic number from the average atomic mass. For bromine (Br), subtract its atomic number (35) from its average atomic mass (79.9) to acquire the average number of neutrons, 44.9.

30. D: Subduction occurs at convergent boundaries. Subduction is the process that occurs when two tectonic plates collide and one plate moves under the other plate.

31. A: The relationship between wavelength and frequency is inversely proportional, and in general, the speed of sound is constant for almost all frequencies. So, the relationship between all three is defined to be: frequency times wavelength is equal to the speed of sound in a given medium, or $f \times \lambda = v$.

32. B: Plutonic, or intrusive, rock forms deep beneath the Earth's surface and cools slowly. Volcanic, or extrusive, rock solidifies at or near the surface. Hypabyssal rock forms below the Earth's surface but not at a depth as great as plutonic rock. Detrital rock is a type of sedimentary rock.

33. A: While landfills are necessary, potential problems include soil contamination, surface water contamination, pollution, and leachate.

34. C: In the stratosphere, temperature increases as altitude increases. The stratosphere contains the ozone layer, which absorbs ultraviolet radiation and then reemits this energy as heat.

35. C: Minerals that form on the sea floor from discarded shells are most likely part of the carbonate class. Minerals that form in karst regions and evaporitic settings may also be carbonates. Examples of minerals in the carbonate class include aragonite, dolomite, calcite, and siderite.

36. A: From highest to lowest: the atlas is cervical vertebra 1, supporting the skull; the axis is cervical vertebra 2; next come cervical vertebrae 3 through 7, the bones in the back of the neck, which are omitted in all choices; then, the 12 thoracic vertebrae are the upper back bones; below these are the 5 lumbar vertebrae in the lower back; the 5 sacral vertebrae (together, the sacrum) are the pelvic and hip-level back bones; and the coccyx or tailbone at the bottom of the spine contains 3-5 small bones, which are often fused together.

37. A: A lysosome is an organelle that is thought to be linked to the aging process and contains digestive enzymes that break down food and unneeded substances. Chromatin is the structure created by DNA and various proteins in the cell's nucleus during interphase and condenses to form chromosomes. Plastids are found in plants and algae. They often contain pigments and usually help make chemical compounds for the plant. The Golgi apparatus prepares macromolecules like proteins and lipids for transport.

38. D: A hypothesis is the use of prior knowledge in order to provide a hypothetical explanation for why something may or may not occur. A hypothesis can be proved wrong or right based on the results of the experiment and repeated trials.

39. B: Total internal reflection occurs when light travels from a denser medium to a rarer medium and the angle of incidence exceeds the critical angle. At the critical angle, the refracted light travels along the boundary (90°), and if the angle of incidence is greater, all the light is reflected into the denser medium; no light is refracted. Therefore, the correct condition is when the angle of incidence is greater than the critical angle.

40. B: When combined, bleach and ammonia can release chlorine gas under certain conditions. Baking soda and vinegar (A) release carbon dioxide gas bubbles. Sugar simply dissolves in water (C). Vinegar (acetic acid) reacts with antacid tablets, producing salt, water, and non-toxic carbon dioxide gas (D). Nothing happens when table salt and rubbing alcohol are mixed (E)—there is no chemical reaction, and the salt does not dissolve.

41. D: Because tropical rainforests lie near the equator, they typically receive 12 hours of intense sunlight on a regular basis; as a result, they are typically warm year-round. None of the other options given describe the primary cause of the heat. Although a forest canopy might indeed help trap heat, for example, the canopy itself is not the actual source of the heat itself; this eliminates option (B). Similarly, although humidity might make the heat seem more intense (due to chemical properties of water), humidity itself is not the cause of heat. This eliminates choice (C). Option (A) can be rejected because it is the sun, not warm ocean currents, that are the principle cause of warmth in tropical rainforests.

42. C: In physics, a systematic error is a consistent difference between the measured value and the true (or accepted) value. Here, all three measurements are 2.1 lb above the true weight of 150 lb, so the systematic error is +2.1 lb. Because all readings are the same to the scale's resolution, the random error is negligible, so it cannot be 2.1 lb and choice A is not correct.

43. B: Some are concerned that by genetically engineering human beings, we will greatly limit our genetic diversity. Some are concerned that only the rich or upper social class will be able to afford genetic engineering, resulting in certain traits eventually being removed from our gene pool. Potential advantages of the genetic engineering of human beings include eradicating diseases, increasing our life span, and eliminating birth defects.

44. A: The eye wall of a hurricane has the strongest winds and the greatest rainfall. The eye wall is the tower-like rim of the eye. It is from this wall that clouds extend out, which are seen from above as the classic outward spiral pattern. A hurricane front is the outermost edge of its influence; although there will be heavy winds and rain in this area, the intensity will be relatively small. The eye of a hurricane is actually a place of surprising peace. In this area, dry and cool air rushes down to the ground or sea. Once there, the air is caught up in the winds of the eye wall and is driven outward at a furious pace.

45. C: Analogous structures do not reveal anything about common ancestors between species. They are simply features that arise due to adapting to similar ecological conditions.

46. C: Acids react with metals like zinc to produce hydrogen gas. Acids turn litmus red, not blue. Acids donate protons, they do not accept them. Acids produce H^+ ions in aqueous solution, not OH^- ions.

47. B: DNA replication begins with a short segment of RNA (not DNA). DNA polymerase cannot begin adding nucleotides without an existing piece of RNA (a primer).

48. B: The shaking that is observed during an earthquake is a direct result of seismic waves. Seismic waves are vibrations that travel through earth when rock slippage along a fault occurs. There are two types of seismic waves: body waves and surface waves. Body waves can either be primary, or P waves, and secondary, or S waves. P waves move more quickly than S waves and create motion that radiates directly outward from the point of origin. S waves produce a shearing, or side-to-side, motion. The other type of seismic wave is a surface wave, which causes much of the shaking felt at Earth's surface.

49. C: Eyewash stations should be capable of delivered rinsing fluid to both eyes for a minimum of 15 minutes. The stations should be located in an accessible area where a person can reach the station in no more than 10 seconds.

50. B: DNA evidence is useful in criminal investigations. Once the DNA is collected, the DNA is extracted or isolated from the sample. Then the DNA is broken into fragments. After that comes DNA electrophoresis, in which the fragments are separated according to size by placing them in a gel and applying a voltage across it. After that, key genetic codes are identified with radioactive markers, and a visual profile is developed. Finally, in DNA profiling, this profile is compared to possible suspects at a crime scene.

51. C: For an experiment to be considered successful, it must yield data that others can reproduce. A reasonable hypothesis (A) may be considered part of a well-designed experiment. A well-written lab report (B) and computer-aided statistical analysis (D) may be considered part of an experiment that is reported on by individuals with expertise.

52. A: Before drawing a conclusion about a hypothesis, one should test it, observe it, and record data about the test results. In the discussion of many scientific papers, scientists will compare and contrast their data to the findings of other groups. The methods of an experiment should be written so an experiment can be replicated.

53. C: In respiration, food is used to produce energy as glucose and oxygen that react to produce carbon dioxide, water and ATP

54. B: Making a determination based on the results of a controlled experiment is a description of concluding. Inferring can be described as explaining or interpreting observations. Reading an instrument during an experiment is one type of quantitative observation. Comparing includes noting similarities and differences.

55. A: Heat between objects in contact with each other is transferred by conduction, choice A. Convection is transfer by currents within a body of fluid, and radiation is the transfer of heat between objects *not* in contact, through light rays emitted by the hotter object and absorbed by the cooler one.

56. C: A chemical change involves a chemical reaction where new products are formed. When silver tarnishes, a thin layer of corrosion is formed, indicating a chemical change. A physical change does not produce new substances. Phase changes such as evaporation and sublimation are examples of physical changes. Salt dissolving in water is also a physical change because the ions just separate, and no new substances are formed.

57. D: Natural selection was Darwin's idea, not Lamarck's. Mendel discovered that genes are the basic units of inheritance. Lamarck's observation about use and disuse is true, although he did not connect it with the underlying mechanism of natural selection.

58. A: Lions live in a wide-open area where there are few large objects to hide behind. In order to get close enough to their prey to chase and attack it, they must be able to sneak up on it. Their coloration is similar to the color of the tall grasses where they live. This allows the lions to blend into their surroundings and get close to their prey.

59. D: Prolonging the life of individuals in a current population will lead to an older age composition. An increased birth rate will cause population growth, but a greater proportion will be younger, not older.

60. A: Anytime there is an accident in the lab, the first step is always to tell the teacher. Even if a student or students were doing something that they should not have been doing, such as horseplay in the lab, the teacher's first priority is still to make sure the students are safe. Telling the teacher will allow him or her to respond appropriately to the situation and make sure that all of the students remain safe.

61. B: Secondary succession occurs when a habitat has been entirely or partially disturbed or destroyed by abandonment, burning, storms, etc.

62. A: Animals of the phylum Mollusca or mollusks, respire (breathe) through gills. Respiration is the process of taking in oxygen and releasing carbon dioxide. Mollusca consists of several classes that include species as diverse as chitons, clams, land and marine snails, and squid. This represents a diverse range of body structures. Many mollusks have a mantle that includes a cavity that is used for both breathing and excretion. Within the mantle are gills (ctenidia). Mollusks do not have tracheas. Some land snails have a respiratory cavity that is often called a lung but is not a true lung. Spiders, which are not mollusks (they are arachnids), have a type of lungs called book lungs. Muscle contraction is not required for the gills to function. Other structures, such as cilia, work to pass water over the gills.

63. C: Unlike the other choices, a tectonic plate shift is a natural geologic process and not a result of human activity. In contrast, human activities are responsible for many forms of ocean destruction. As wetlands are degraded or lost, many ecosystems and species are also lost, interrupting their respective food webs. Food webs within the oceans are further disrupted by pollution and climate change, which alter water temperatures and conditions. The diminishment of coral reefs reduces the ocean's natural water filtration and destroys critical habitats used for breeding and feeding.

64. A: A model volcano eruption using vinegar and baking soda is an acid-base reaction, not an oxidation-reduction reaction. Tin cans are steel cans with a tin coating. Applying this coating involves an oxidation-reduction reaction. Decomposition of hydrogen peroxide and dough rising through the production of CO_2 by yeast are both redox reactions. Rust forming on a steel fence is a redox reaction.

65. A: The center of an atom is known as the nucleus. It is composed of protons and neutrons. The nucleus is positively charged due to protons having a positive charge and neutrons being electrically neutral.

66. C: The independent variable is the variable that is changed in the experiment in order to determine its effect on the dependent variable or the outcome of the experiment. The dependent variable results from the experimenter making only one change to an experiment that can be repeated with the same results. Mrs. Jones's class was comparing the effects of sugar and artificial sweetener on the overall color of cookies once they are baked; thus, the one thing that should be changed in the experiment is the sugar and artificial sweetener in the recipe. All of the other ingredients stay the same. For the experiment to be valid and not influenced by any other variables, the students should keep the temperature and baking time the same, as these could affect the color of the cookies as well.

67. A: Anthophyta is a division of plants that produces seeds as part of reproduction. Spermatopyta is the broader group that includes all plants that produce seeds for reproduction, which includes gymnosperms and angiosperms (the same group as anthophyta). Anthophyta are also known as the group that contains flowering plants. It is the largest and most diverse grouping of plants and includes many food, clothing, and medicinal uses for humans. Grains, beans, nuts, fruits, vegetables, spices, tea, coffee, chocolate, cotton, linen, and aspirin are all derived from plants from anthophyta. Lycophyta is a small group of plants including club mosses and scale trees. Sphenophyta contains about thirty species including horsetails, foxtails, or scouring rushes. Pterophyta contains non-seed plants like ferns. Lycophyta, sphenophyta, and pterophyta all use spores to reproduce sexually.

68. A: Observation includes collecting evidence, using the five senses, and writing descriptions. Classifying includes grouping items based on similarities, differences, and interrelationships. Inferring includes explaining or interpreting collected evidence. Communication is reporting to others what has been found by experimentation.

69. B: Since the mountain in the figure has the oldest rock in its core and the youngest rock in its outer layers, it is best described as an anticline. Any mountain that results from a crustal fold and has an upward, convex shape is called an antiform. Mountains in which the rocks are progressively older from the outer layers to the core are anticlines. Synclines have downward, or concave, folds, and fault-block mountains result when faults in continental crust cause certain sections to lift or tilt. Grabens are a formation associated with fault-block mountains.

70. D: Although data from previous trials is important for the final lab report and results summary, it is not important for the current trial being tested. A final summary will incorporate all trial data results and observations in order to determine a final conclusion about the results. Temperature, color changes, and the production of a gas or odor indicate that a chemical change has occurred and should be recorded as an observation.

71. D: The complete Punnett square is shown below.

	B	**b**
B	BB	Bb
b	Bb	bb

Because male-pattern baldness is a recessive gene, the offspring would need the *bb* gene combination in order to inherit this trait. Possibility 4 corresponds to the *bb* gene combination.

72. B: Ohm's Law states that voltage and current in an electrical circuit are directly proportional to one another. Ohm's Law can be expressed as $V = IR$, where V is voltage, I is current and R is resistance. Voltage is also known as electrical potential difference and is the force that moves electrons through a circuit. For a given amount of resistance, an increase in voltage will result in an increase in current. Resistance and current are inversely proportional to each other. For a given voltage, an increase in resistance will result in a decrease in current.

73. C: Physical weathering of rocks can be caused by changes in temperature and pressure, as well as the freezing and thawing of water on the surfaces of rocks. Oxidation is a chemical process, not a physical one. Therefore, it is considered an example of chemical rather than physical weathering.

74. D: A covalent bond is one in which atoms share valence electrons. Within a water molecule, one oxygen atom and two hydrogen atoms share valence electrons to yield the H_2O structure.

75. C: Overgrazing and deforestation directly contribute to soil erosion by destroying the natural ground cover that normally prevents soil from being washed and blown away. These activities can ultimately result in desertification, which renders land unsuitable for agriculture.

76. B: It is true that galaxies are gravitationally bound, so that structures within them orbit around the center. Galaxies do contain dark matter, and only the largest "giant" galaxies contain over one trillion stars. The smallest "dwarf" galaxies contain as few as 10 million stars. Clusters and superclusters are composed of many galaxies.

77. D: The field of stratigraphy is divided into several subfields, each of which focuses on a unique aspect of sedimentary material and yields unique insights about the material's age. In the subfield of chronostratigraphy, a material's age is estimated by determining when it was formed or deposited. The study of the vertical layering of rock types is called lithostratigraphy, and the study of fossil ages in rock layers is called biostratigraphy. Magnetostratigraphy examines data about changes in detrital remanent magnetism (DRM) at the time rocks were formed.

78. A: Many organisms, especially organisms that live in harsh conditions such as deserts or frozen icy areas, have developed specific adaptations that allow them to survive. For example, cacti are able to expand to store large amounts of water, coyotes absorb some water from their food, and snakes can escape the heat by hiding within rocks.

79. A: Solutions and compounds used in labs may be hazardous according to state and local regulatory agencies and should be treated with appropriate precaution. Emptying the solutions into the sink and rinsing with warm water and soap does not take into account the hazards associated with a specific solution in terms of vapors or interactions with water, soap, and waste piping systems. Ensuring the solutions are secured in closed containers and throwing them away may allow toxic chemicals into landfills and subsequently into freshwater systems. Storing the solutions in a secured, dry place for later use is incorrect, as chemicals should not be reused due to the possibility of contamination.

80. B: Unlike other organic molecules, lipids are not water soluble. They are largely nonpolar, and therefore hydrophobic. Lipids are not built from repeating monomers; this is characteristic of carbohydrates, proteins, and amino acids. Enzymes are proteins that can catalyze reactions. Lipids store more energy per gram than carbohydrates and proteins.

81. B: Currently, there is no vaccine and no cure for HIV. HIV continues to mutate and evolve unchecked; however, the progression from HIV to AIDS can be controlled by antiretroviral drugs.

82. C: The loss of biodiversity destabilizes ecosystems and impacts society by decreasing the food supply, decreasing the access to raw materials and clean water, and increasing the vulnerability to natural disasters.

83. D: Refraction is the process whereby the speed of light is changed as it passes from one transparent medium, like air, to another, like water. The change in speed bends the light wave. Scattering (A) is the process whereby light bounces back at multiple angles when it strikes a rough or uneven surface (instead of bouncing back at a single angle as when it strikes a smooth surface). When light bounces back off a surface, this is reflection (C). Materials that do not reflect *any* light waves (smoothly or scattered) or refract any light waves appear opaque (i.e., we cannot see through them) because they take in all frequencies of light; this is absorption (B).

84. D: A good hypothesis must be testable. This means it may be proved or disproved by testing using a controlled experiment. A controlled experiment may have several constants but only one independent variable.

85. A: The control in an experiment is not subject to the variable being tested—in this case, the new drug. The volunteers who are given the drug comprise the experimental group.

86. C: The pH probes should be stored according to the manufacturer's instructions. In general, pH probes should never be stored in water or stored dry without first draining the electrode. They should always be stored in an appropriate buffer or reference electrolyte, which is usually a 3M – 4M potassium chloride solution.

87. C: This can be read from the graph. The mesosphere has the coldest temperatures in the atmospheric regions beneath outer space. Beyond the upper limits of the mesosphere, the thermosphere gets progressively hotter. However, it is worth noting that even though the temperature gets really high, the density of molecules and atoms is so low that it would not feel very hot.

88. D: The drug company has provided all of the same variables to the two groups with the exception of one group receiving the drug and the other taking the placebo. The group on the drug is experimental; the placebo is a control group.

89. A: The average distance from the earth to the sun is equal to one astronomical unit (AU). An AU is equal to 93 million miles and is far smaller than a light-year or a parsec. A light-year is defined as the distance light can travel in a vacuum in one year, and is equal to roughly 63,241 AU. A parsec is the parallax of one arcsecond and is equal to 2.0626×10^5 astronomical units.

90. D: Operons are common in prokaryotes. They are units of DNA that control the transcription of DNA and code for their own regulatory proteins as well as structural proteins.

91. A: A magnetic field is created by a spin magnetic dipole moment and the orbital magnetic dipole moment of the electrons in atoms. Therefore, it is the spinning and rotating of electrons in atoms that creates a magnetic field. The separation of charged particles in atoms describes the nucleus and electron clouds within an atom. The vibrational and translational motion of atoms creates thermal energy. Loosely held valence electrons surrounding an atom indicates a good electrical conductor.

92. B: Glass cleaner traditionally was a 5% ammonia solution. Recently most glass cleaners are more environmentally friendly solutions containing much less ammonia. Bleach is a solution of 3-6% sodium hypochlorite.

93. A: Igneous rocks form from the solidification of molten rock; metamorphic rocks form from changes in heat, pressure, or chemical activity; and sedimentary rocks are formed mainly by the compaction of rock fragments and other materials. All three types of rock may vary in texture, age, and mineral content.

94. A: In the ecosystem described, birds eat beetles, crickets, and grasshoppers. If a pesticide were to kill off part of the beetle population, birds would be forced to consume more crickets and grasshoppers to meet their energy needs. As a result, there would be a decrease in the cricket population.

95. D: Ozone layer depletion results in higher UV levels reaching the earth. These higher levels of UV rays may result in more skin cancer, sunburn, and premature aging of skin, damage to marine life such as plankton, and decreased crop yields of wheat, corn, and soybeans. However, the higher concentration of UV light has increased the amount of vitamin D synthesized in humans.

96. A: Three ways of transmitting heat are conduction (A), convection (B), and radiation (C). When heat is transmitted through solids, this is done via conduction. Conduction occurs between solid materials directly contacting one another. Convection (B) is how heat travels through liquids and gases. Heat makes them expand, lowering their density so they rise. When they cool, they recover density and fall. This heating-rising and cooling-falling process creates a current known as convection. Radiation (C), like the heat from the sun, occurs when electromagnetic waves travel through space and transfer heat to objects, like the Earth, that they touch. Therefore, (D) is incorrect.

97. B: The most severe mass extinction event in Earth's history was the Permian-Triassic Event. It occurred approximately 251.4 million years ago, and resulted in the extinction of 96 percent of all marine species and 70 percent of terrestrial vertebrate species.

98. A: Glass is manufactured and can be recycled, but is considered a non-renewable resource. Wood is considered a renewable resource because with proper management, an equilibrium can be reached between harvesting trees and planting new ones. Cattle are managed in herds and a balance can be achieved between those consumed and those born. Soil is the result of long-term erosion and includes organic matter and minerals needed by plants. Soil found naturally in the environment is renewed. Crops can be rotated to help maintain a healthy soil composition for farming.

99. B: When more than one gene contributes to a trait, inheritance of that trait is said to be polygenic. This type of inheritance does not follow the rules of Mendelian genetics. Pleiotropy is the opposite, which one gene contributes to two or more unrelated traits. Codominace is a non-Mendelian inheritance where both alleles are expressed in a heterozygote individual, rather than the dominant allele being expressed and the recessive being masked. Gene linkage occurs between two genes that are located near each other on a chromosome and are usually inherited together.

100. D: A lunar eclipse occurs when the full moon moves through the Earth's shadow. A solar eclipse occurs when a new moon passes between the Earth and the Sun.

Practice Test #2

1. What other planet in the solar system experiences a greenhouse effect similar to that observed on Earth?

a. Mercury
b. Venus
c. Neptune
d. Saturn

2. Given the chemical reaction $4\ Al(s) + 3\ O_2(g) \rightarrow 2\ Al_2O_3(s)$, how many moles of $O_2(g)$ are needed to produce 100.0 moles of $Al_2O_3(s)$?

a. 100.0
b. 150.0
c. 200.0
d. 250.0

3. Which of the following was the first widespread use of X-rays?

a. Medical imaging
b. Fighting cancer
c. Security scanners
d. Discovering distant galaxies

4. Which of the following is NOT a characteristic of scientific inquiry?

a. Continual posing of questions and testing of hypotheses
b. Objective analysis of experimental data
c. Ongoing peer review of shared information
d. The assumption that published literature is accurate and unbiased

5. Which of the following events directly results in a volcanic eruption?

a. A batholith forms beneath the Earth's surface.
b. Magma fills vertical and horizontal fractures in the Earth's crust, creating sills and dikes.
c. An oceanic plate is subducted by a continental plate.
d. A dike reaches the Earth's surface, and a plume passes through it.

6. Which of the following statements about the Moon is NOT true?

a. Only one side of the Moon is seen from Earth.
b. The Moon only rotates once in one orbit around the Earth.
c. The Moon is slowly moving closer to the Earth.
d. The gravitational acceleration on the surface of the Moon is approximately one-sixth of the gravitational acceleration on the surface of the Earth.

7. A long nail is heated at one end. After a few seconds, the other end of the nail becomes equally hot. What type of heat transfer does this represent?

a. Radiation
b. Conduction
c. Convection
d. Entropy

8. Which of the following is a serious direct impact of climate change?

a. Soil erosion
b. Deforestation
c. Water pollution
d. Increase in average sea level

9. The combination of DNA with histones is called

a. A centromere
b. Chromatin
c. A chromatid
d. Nucleoli

10. Which statement best explains the Biological Species Concept (BSC)?

a. It states that the status of species is based on the ability to pass on the most successful traits to their offspring.
b. It states that the status of species is based on the reproductive isolation of populations.
c. It states that the status of species is based on the ability of populations to mix and produce fertile hybrids.
d. It states that the status of a species is due to the theory of natural selection.

11. A gas at constant volume is cooled. Which statement about the gas must be true?

a. The kinetic energy of the gas molecules has decreased.
b. The gas has condensed to a liquid.
c. The weight of the gas has decreased.
d. The density of the gas has increased.

12. Which of the following is an example of chemical weathering?

a. Rain freezing on the roadway
b. Ivy growing on the side of a wooden house
c. Vinegar fizzing when poured on a rock
d. A river carrying sediment downstream

13. Which of the following statements is NOT true about the period of a simple pendulum?

a. As the mass of a pendulum increases, the period increases.
b. For small amplitudes, the period of a pendulum is approximately independent of amplitude.
c. A pendulum swings more slowly at higher elevation.
d. To double the period of a pendulum, the length must be quadrupled.

14. A normal human sperm must contain:

a. An X chromosome
b. A Y chromosome
c. 23 chromosomes
d. Both an X and a Y chromosome

15. What lab equipment would most likely be used to measure a liquid solution?

a. Flask
b. Triple beam balance
c. Graduated cylinder
d. Test tube

16. The data below was collected by repeating the same experiment four different times. What conclusion can be drawn based on the data shown?

Bicycle Obstacle Race

Student	Trial 1	Trial 2	Trial 3	Trial 4
Kayla	57.6 s	37.6 s	37.3 s	36.2 s
Carson	64.0 s	32.6 s	31.2 s	28.4 s
Jeremy	59.2 s	31.0 s	28.8 s	27.9 s
Rachel	61.3 s	42.6 s	39.5 s	39.0 s

a. The data was accurate in all four trials
b. The data in trials 2 through 4 is probably inaccurate
c. An error occurred in trial 1 that gave inaccurate data
d. The times in trial 4 are fastest because the students were tired

17. Once a hypothesis has been verified and accepted, it becomes which of the following?

a. A fact
b. A law
c. A conclusion
d. A theory

18. What do all animals belonging to the Echinodermata phylum have in common?

a. They use multiple appendages for locomotion.
b. They use tube feet for locomotion and feeding.
c. They have an exoskeleton made of chitin.
d. They must shed their outer layer of skin to grow.

Refer to the following for question 19:

Let B represent the dominant allele for a full head of hair, and let b represent the recessive allele for male-pattern baldness. The following Punnett square represents the offspring of two people with recessive genes for baldness.

	B	b
B	Possibility 1	Possibility 2
b	Possibility 3	Possibility 4

19. According to the Punnett square, which possibility would produce an offspring with a full head of hair?

a. Possibility 1
b. Possibility 2
c. Possibility 3
d. All of the above

20. Two cars driving in opposite directions collide. If you ignore friction and any other outside interactions, which of the following statements is always true?

a. The total momentum is conserved.
b. The sum of the potential and kinetic energy is conserved.
c. The total velocity of the cars is conserved.
d. The total impulse is conserved.

21. Which of the following does NOT display an appropriate or safe use of chemicals?

a. Never taste any chemicals.
b. To test odors, waft the odors towards your nose with a cupped hand.
c. Never return unused chemicals to the stock bottle.
d. When diluting acids, always pour the water into the acid.

22. Fossils are least likely to be found in which type of rock?

a. Sedimentary rock
b. Metamorphic rock
c. Igneous rock
d. Fossils are commonly found in all types of rock

23. Which of the following types of chemicals are considered generally unsafe to store together?

I. Liquids and solids
II. Acids and bases
III. Reducing agents and oxidizing agents
IV. Metals and salts

a. I, II
b. II, III
c. III, IV
d. I, IV

24. A student is working on a science project and is going through each step of the scientific method. After the student conducts his or her first experiment and records the results of the experimental test, what should the student do next?

a. Communicate the results.
b. Draw a conclusion.
c. Repeat the experiment.
d. Create a hypothesis.

25. The structure of the Milky Way galaxy is best described as:

a. Spiral
b. Starburst
c. Elliptical
d. Irregular

26. What effect does science have on technology?

a. Science verifies what technology discovers
b. Technology often results from scientific discoveries
c. Science has no effect on technology; each is independent of the other
d. Scientific progress is dependent on technology

27. The Coriolis effect in the Earth's oceans is caused by:

a. The Earth's rotation
b. The Earth's magnetic field
c. Variations in the density of seawater
d. The Gulf Stream

Refer to the following for question 28:

Diagram of a complete, perfect flower

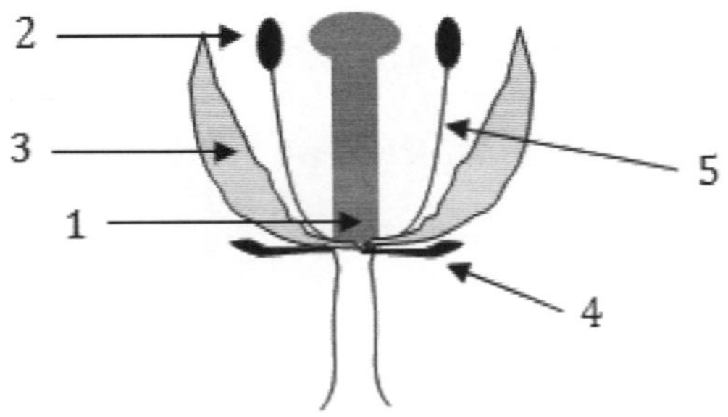

28. The structure in which microspores are produced is:

a. 1
b. 2
c. 3
d. 4

29. What is the role of ribosomes?

a. Protein production
b. Waste removal
c. Transport
d. Storage

30. The process that causes lithospheric plates to move over the surface of the mantle is called:

a. Conduction
b. Convection
c. Tension
d. Subduction

31. What type of mutation is represented by the following sequence?

Original: 1 2 3 4 5 6
Mutated: 1 5 4 3 2 6

a. Breakage
b. Deletion
c. Insertion
d. Inversion

32. Which of the following plant organelles contain the pigment that gives green leaves their color?

a. Centrioles
b. Cell walls
c. Chloroplasts
d. Central vacuole

33. What characteristic of electromagnetic radiation determines if it is classified as a radio wave or an x-ray?

a. Intensity
b. Phase angle
c. Wavelength
d. Speed of light

34. Scientists often form hypotheses based on particular observations. Which of the following is NOT true of a good hypothesis?

a. A good hypothesis is complex.
b. A good hypothesis is testable.
c. A good hypothesis is logical.
d. A good hypothesis predicts future events.

35. An inch is approximately equivalent to which of the following?

a. 25.4 mm
b. 25.4 cm
c. 2.54×10^{-4} km
d. 2.54×10^{2} m

36. Balance the following reaction between sulfuric acid and aluminum hydroxide by filling in the correct stoichiometric values for each chemical.

$$\_\ H_2SO_4 + \_\ Al(OH)_3 \rightarrow \_\ Al_2(SO_4)_3 + \_\ H_2O$$

a. 3, 2, 1, 6
b. 2, 3, 1, 3
c. 3, 3, 2, 6
d. 1, 2, 1, 4

37. What preventative safety equipment is required when working with flammable materials?

a. Apron
b. Fire blanket and extinguisher
c. Eye wash station
d. Goggles

38. In a food chain, where does energy go after the secondary consumer dies?

a. Back to the Sun
b. To the producers
c. Into the air, becoming wind
d. To decomposers

39. World weather patterns are most influenced by which of the following?

a. Wind belts
b. The Earth's orbit
c. Ocean currents
d. Atmospheric conditions

40. Which of the following cell types has a peptidoglycan cell wall?

a. Algae
b. Bacteria
c. Fungi
d. Land plants

41. Which of the following is NOT an environmental impact of an irrigation scheme that draws water from a river?

a. Reduction in the downstream river discharge
b. Raising of the level of the water table
c. Decreased evaporation in the area
d. Increased drainage flow

42. A bacterial mini-chromosome used in recombinant DNA technology is called a

a. Centromere
b. Telomere
c. Plasmid
d. Transposon

43. When two tectonic plates are moving laterally in opposing directions, this is called a(n):

a. Transform boundary
b. Compressional boundary
c. Oppositional boundary
d. Lateral boundary

44. DNA replication occurs during which of the following phases?

a. Prophase I
b. Prophase II
c. Interphase I
d. Interphase II

Refer to the following for question 45:

Many fishermen will watch the tide report for the local area and get up very early or stay out late in order to have the best fishing opportunity. One night while out late fishing, a fisherman noticed that the land temperature cooled rapidly, while the ocean water stayed relatively warm.

45. Which factor affects the fisherman's fishing opportunities?

a. The gravitational relationship between the earth and moon
b. The gravitational relationship between the earth and sun
c. The earth's gravity
d. The moon's phases

46. Which of the following diseases has been eradicated by immunization?

a. Polio
b. Mumps
c. Measles
d. Smallpox

47. When metamorphic rock is stressed unevenly during recrystallization, it can result in:

a. Foliation
b. Contact metamorphism
c. Regional metamorphism
d. Extrusion

48. Which of the following is the greatest ethical controversy related to in vitro fertilization?

a. The fertilization outside of the mother's body
b. The multiple eggs produced by the ovary
c. The expense involved
d. The disposal of unused zygotes or embryos

49. Which of the following is correct regarding how objects produce sound and how we hear it?

a. Sound is something that causes vibrations in the air.
b. Sound waves are vibrations disturbing media like air.
c. Sound causes vibrations in the air but not in the ear.
d. Sound is the same energy type in the ear and brain.

50. The lithification process results in the formation of which of the following types of rocks?

a. Sedimentary
b. Intrusive igneous
c. Extrusive igneous
d. Metamorphic

51. James Hutton is best known for:

a. Establishing the first observable evidence for the Big Bang Theory
b. Suggesting the Third Law of Thermodynamics
c. Proposing the theory of uniformitarianism
d. Introducing the Law of Superposition

52. Hund's rule regarding electronic configuration states:

a. Electrons in the same orbital must have an opposite spin.
b. Electrons must fill lower energy orbitals before filling higher energy orbitals.
c. Electrons must populate empty orbitals of equal energy before filling occupied orbitals.
d. Electrons must have the same nuclear spin as the nucleus.

53. Which of the following creates an electromagnet?

a. Rapidly spinning and rotating electrons inside an iron bar
b. An iron bar moving inside a coil of wire that contains a current
c. The movement of electrons through a complete circuit
d. Convection currents within the liquid core of Earth's interior

54. Which of the following materials has randomly aligned dipoles?

a. A non-magnetic substance
b. An electromagnet
c. A permanent magnet
d. A horseshoe magnet

55. Which of the following is true concerning the benefits of radiation therapy?

a. Radiation therapy cannot be used to reduce pain.
b. Radiation therapy is given only to shrink tumors.
c. Radiation therapy kills only cancer cells.
d. Radiation therapy kills cancer cells by damaging their DNA.

56. The electrolysis of water is an example of which of the following?

a. An adiabatic process
b. A chemical change
c. A synthesis reaction
d. Reverse osmosis

57. Which of the following is a solute?

a. Salt in a mixture of salt and pepper
b. Air in a mixture of ash and air
c. Water in a mixture of salt and water
d. Sugar in a mixture of sugar and water

58. When using a microscope, which objective provides the greatest field of view?

a. 4X
b. 10X
c. 40X
d. 100X

59. Which of the following is NOT an impact of strip mining of coal?

a. Destruction of landscapes, forest, and wildlife habitats
b. Dust and noise pollution
c. Chemical contamination of groundwater
d. Lowering of the water table

60. The energy flow through an ecosystem is represented by an energy pyramid. In the energy pyramid for a terrestrial ecosystem, the producers utilize 6,000 kilocalories per square meter per year. What approximate amount of energy is transferred to the third trophic level of this ecosystem?

a. 0.6 kilocalories per square meter per year
b. 6 kilocalories per square meter per year
c. 60 kilocalories per square meter per year
d. 600 kilocalories per square meter per year

61. Which of the following historical figures is NOT correctly matched with his contribution to modern science?

a. Louis Pasteur and the germ concept of disease
b. Thomas Edison and the theory of relativity
c. Johannes Kepler and the laws of planetary motion
d. Nicolaus Copernicus and the heliocentric view of the solar system

62. Which graph segment below represents the greatest acceleration?

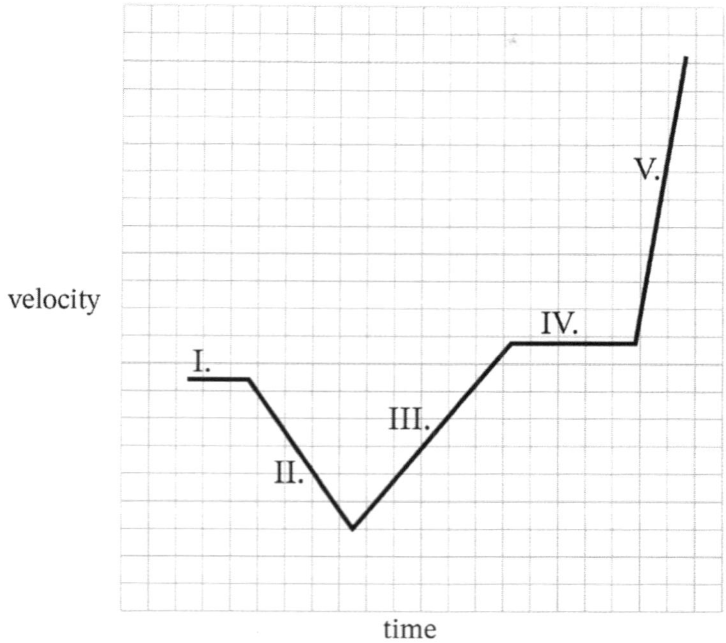

a. II
b. III
c. V
d. III and V

63. Limestone is one example of which subtype of sedimentary rock?

a. Clastic
b. Volcanic
c. Biochemical
d. Pegmatite

64. During primary succession, which species would most likely be a pioneer species?

a. Lichens
b. Fir trees
c. Mosquitoes
d. Dragonflies

65. Which of the following molecules is thought to have acted as the first enzyme in early life on earth?

a. Protein
b. RNA
c. DNA
d. Triglycerides

66. What unit describes the loudness of a sound?

a. Hertz (Hz)
b. Decibels (dB)
c. Meters (m)
d. Meters per second (m/s)

67. What are pure substances that consist of more than one type of atom?

a. Elements
b. Compounds
c. Molecules
d. Mixtures

68. Which color of light has the highest frequency?

a. Blue
b. Red
c. Green
d. Violet

69. Which of the following is an example of a descriptive study?

a. Comparing the average height of male vs female penguins of a particular species
b. Investigating the growth rate of fungi in various synthetic media
c. Testing the effectiveness of a drug with a double-blind study
d. Split-testing the impact on sales of a new description of menu items.

70. All of the following are examples of metamorphic rocks EXCEPT:

a. Granite
b. Quartzite
c. Slate
d. Marble

71. A liquid is heated from 50 °C to 80 °C. Which of the following statements is generally true about the solubility of solids and gases in the liquid?

a. The solubility of solids will increase, and the solubility of gases will decrease.
b. The solubility of solids will decrease, and the solubility of gases will increase.
c. The solubility of solids will increase, and the solubility of gases will increase.
d. The solubility of solids will decrease, and the solubility of gases will decrease.

72. Of the following actions, which best represents the science process skill of Inference?

a. Formulating new hypotheses based on experimental results
b. Finding patterns and meaning in the results of experiments
c. Identifying properties of things/situations using the senses
d. Reporting experimental results and conclusions to others

73. Which of the following is a vector quantity?

a. Distance
b. Speed
c. Velocity
d. Time

74. Two balances in a classroom laboratory are used to determine the mass of an object. The actual mass of the object is 15.374 grams.

Measurement	Triple Beam Balance	Digital Balance
1	15.38 grams	15.375 grams
2	15.39 grams	15.376 grams
3	15.37 grams	15.376 grams
4	15.38 grams	15.375 grams

Which of the following statements is true concerning the accuracy and precision of these two balances?

a. The triple beam balance is both more accurate and more precise.
b. The triple beam balance is more accurate, but the digital balance is more precise.
c. The digital balance is more accurate, but the triple beam balance is more precise.
d. The digital balance is both more accurate and more precise.

75. Two companion models, gradualism and punctuated equilibrium, dominate evolutionary theory. Which of the following statements is most consistent with the theory of punctuated equilibrium?

a. Fossils show changes over large periods of time.
b. Fossils showing intermediate characteristics may not necessarily be found.
c. Speciation occurs gradually.
d. Evolution is a slow, steady process.

76. Which of the following is a disadvantage of fossil fuels?

a. Extraction processes are extremely dangerous.
b. There is no way to control pollution from their processing.
c. They are difficult to store safely.
d. Their use contributes to global warming.

77. The following is the anticodon sequence formed during translation. What is the mRNA codon sequence?

A C G U A C G C U

a. T G C A T G C G A
b. U G C T U G C G T
c. U G C A U G C G A
d. U C G A U C G C A

78. Graham's law is best used to determine what relationship between two different materials?

a. Pressure and volume
b. Volume and temperature
c. Mass and diffusion rate
d. Diffusion rate and temperature

79. What property of light explains why a pencil in a glass of water appears to be bent?

a. Reflection
b. Refraction
c. Angle of incidence = angle of reflection
d. Constructive interference

80. Which of the following is the major way in which carbon is released into the environment?

a. Transpiration
b. Respiration
c. Fixation
d. Sedimentation

81. Which of the following lessons would be the best set of examples illustrating the difference between scientific fact and theory?

a. Big Bang and Laws of Motion
b. Chaos theory and Evolution
c. Conservation of Mass/Electricity and Carbon-14 Dating
d. Astronomical Wormholes and Black Holes

82. Methylmercury is a toxin produced indirectly from what energy source?

a. Oil
b. Natural gas
c. Wood
d. Coal

83. The amount of potential energy an object has depends on all of the following except its

a. Mass
b. Height above ground
c. Gravitational attraction
d. Temperature

84. Water that evaporates from oceans can precipitate over land due to the process of:

a. Transpiration
b. Advection
c. Sublimation
d. Interception

85. When the accumulation of snow and ice exceeds ablation, which of the following occurs as a direct result?

a. An iceberg breaks free from a glacier.
b. A glacier gradually forms.
c. A glacier slowly erodes.
d. A lake forms within a glacier.

86. Which of the following are formed when the plasma membrane surrounds a particle outside of the cell?

a. Golgi bodies
b. Rough endoplasmic reticulum
c. Secretory vesicles
d. Endocytic vesicles

87. Plant A undergoes C4 photosynthesis. What type of environment would the plant most likely live in?

a. Plant A lives in a very cold environment.
b. Plant A lives in a very hot environment.
c. Plant A lives in a marine environment.
d. Plant A lives in a dark environment that lacks solar energy.

88. A boy is outside in the winter and notices that he begins shivering when he gets cold. A girl is outside during the summer and begins sweating when she gets hot. Why do the children's bodies react this way?

a. The children's bodies are attempting to regulate their temperature.
b. The children's bodies are trying to fight off disease.
c. The children's bodies are reacting to the amount of sunlight or shade.
d. The children are having an allergic reaction to something in the air.

89. What are goggles, lab aprons, and gloves called?

a. People protective equines
b. Personal protect equipment
c. Personal protective equipment
d. People protective equipment

90. Which of the following statements correctly describes a difference between the lithosphere and the asthenosphere?

a. The asthenosphere is composed of atmospheric gas, while the lithosphere is composed of liquids and solids.
b. The asthenosphere is hotter and more fluid than the lithosphere.
c. The lithosphere is hotter and has a different chemical composition than the asthenosphere.
d. Heat is transferred through conduction in the asthenosphere, while it is transferred through convection in the lithosphere.

91. Burning fossil fuels releases sulfur dioxide and nitrogen dioxide. These pollutants lead to which environmental problem?

a. Denitrification
b. Acid rain
c. Global climate change
d. Ozone depletion

92. Which of the following is false regarding solar energy?

a. Solar energy is environmentally friendly
b. Solar energy has the greatest conversion efficiency
c. Solar energy is low maintenance
d. Solar energy is silent

93. Which of the following processes is NOT part of the formation of sedimentary rock?

a. Layering
b. Cementation
c. Compaction
d. Heat

94. What does it mean when someone says that electric charge is conserved?

a. Like charges repel, and unlike charges attract.
b. The net charge of an isolated system remains constant.
c. Charges come from electrons and protons.
d. Charge can never be created or destroyed.

95. Which of the following statements best describes the physical structure of the universe?

a. Galaxies are the largest structures in the universe, and they are distributed evenly throughout space.
b. Superclusters are the largest structures in the universe, and they are distributed evenly throughout space.
c. Superclusters are the largest structures in the universe, and they are unevenly distributed so that large voids exist in space.
d. Filaments are the largest structures in the universe, and they surround large, bubble-like voids.

Refer to the following for question 96:

> *A student is conducting an experiment using a ball that is attached to the end of a string, forming a pendulum. The student pulls the ball back so that it is at an angle to its resting position. As the student releases the ball, it swings forward and backward. The student measures the time it takes the ball to make one complete period. A period is defined as the time it takes the ball to swing forward and back again to its starting position. This is repeated using different string lengths.*

96. The student formed the following hypothesis:

> *Lengthening the string of the pendulum will increase the time it takes the ball to make one complete period.*

What correction would you have the student make to the hypothesis to make it follow the classical hypothesis model?

a. Turn it into an "if/then" statement.
b. Change "will increase" to "increases."
c. Switch the order of the sentence so that the phrase about the period comes first, and the phrase about the string's length is last.
d. No corrections are needed.

97. Which of the following best describes Earth's atmosphere?

a. 25% nitrogen, 55% oxygen, 20% water vapor and other gases
b. 78% nitrogen, 21% oxygen, 1% water vapor and other gases
c. 38% nitrogen, 60% oxygen, 2% water vapor and other gases
d. 90% nitrogen, 5% oxygen, 5% water vapor and other gases

98. Darwin's idea that evolution occurs by the gradual accumulation of small changes can be described as:

a. Punctuated equilibrium
b. Phyletic gradualism
c. Convergent evolution
d. Adaptive radiation

99. What is the most common type of volcano on Earth?

a. Lava dome
b. Composite volcano
c. Shield volcano
d. Cinder cone

100. Which statement best explains the importance of recycling and using alternative sources of energy?

a. It will lead to greater production of goods and consumer spending in the future.
b. It will benefit the health and safety of populations and the long-term sustainability of the environment.
c. It will get rid of human disease and end economic warfare in the future.
d. It will allow fossil fuel supplies to be replenished for their continued use in the future.

Answer Key and Explanations for Test #2

1. B: Venus experiences a greenhouse effect similar to that observed on Earth as its dense atmosphere traps the solar radiation and creates a greenhouse effect. The greenhouse gases, including ozone, carbon dioxide, water vapor, and methane, trap infrared radiation that is reflected back toward the atmosphere. While both Venus and Earth experience the greenhouse effect, Venus's greenhouse effect is much more severe. Earth, on the other hand, has many more natural convective processes that help move carbon and other gases around, tempering the effect some. Human activity produces byproducts that contribute to the greenhouse effect. Some practices that increase the amount of greenhouse gases are burning natural gas and oil; farming, which leads to more methane and nitrous oxide; deforestation, which decreases the amount of offset oxygen; and population growth in general, which increases the volume of greenhouse gases. Increased gases mean more infrared radiation is trapped. While the greenhouse effect is not itself debated, the long-term effects tend to be hotly debated among scientists and in political agendas.

2. B: The coefficients of the balanced chemical equation can be used to form a mole ratio to be used in dimensional analysis. Since 3 moles of O_2 produce 2 moles of Al_2O_3, the needed mole ratio is $\left(\frac{3 \text{ mol } O_2}{2 \text{ mol } Al_2O_3}\right)$. Using dimensional analysis, $(100.0 \text{ mol } Al_2O_3)\left(\frac{3 \text{ mol } O_2}{2 \text{ mol } Al_2O_3}\right)$ requires 150.0 moles O_2.

3. A: X-rays were put to clinical use within a month of their discovery to image bone fractures and foreign objects in the body. Later, they were used to locate tumors and to fight cancer. Distant galaxies have been discovered by the detection of X-rays from stars. X-rays are commonly used as security scanners.

4. D: Not all scientific literature is reliable. Students must learn to distinguish between sources that are consistent with experimental evidence and those that are biased or misleading in their conclusions. Scientists study one another's work to direct and support original research, but they recognize that interpretations of data may vary and that existing theories are always subject to testing and revision.

5. D: A volcano occurs when a dike (a vertical fracture in the Earth's crust that fills with magma) reaches the Earth's surface and a plume (a spurt of magma) passes through it. Batholiths are large masses of igneous rock that form beneath the Earth's surface, and a sill is a horizontal fracture in the Earth's crust that fills with magma. When an oceanic plate is subducted by a continental plate, it results in the formation of mountain ranges and volcanic arcs.

6. C: The Moon is slowly moving further away from the Earth. The Moon is moving a little less than 4 cm a year away from the Earth. Since the Moon only rotates once in every orbit around the Earth, the same side is always seen from Earth. The acceleration of gravity on the surface of the Moon is approximately one-sixth of the gravitational acceleration on the surface of the Earth. Although the Moon has less than 1/80 the mass of the Earth, it also has a smaller radius, and the acceleration of gravity on the surface depends on both.

7. B: A long nail or other type of metal, substance, or matter that is heated at one end and then the other end becomes equally hot is an example of conduction. Conduction is energy transfer by neighboring molecules from an area of hotter temperature to cooler temperature. Radiation (A), or thermal radiation, refers to heat being transferred through empty space by electromagnetic radiation. An example is sunlight heating the earth. Convection (C) refers to heat being transferred by molecules moving from one location in the substance to another creating a heat current, usually in a gas or a liquid. Entropy (D) relates to the second law of thermodynamics and refers to how much heat or energy is no longer available to do work in a system. It can also be stated as the amount of disorder in a system.

8. D: Of these options, the only real direct impact of climate change is the rising sea level. This is due to the melting glaciers and ice sheets. Also, the oceans expand slightly as they get warmer.

9. B: DNA wrapped around histone proteins is called chromatin. In a eukaryotic cell, DNA is always associated with protein; it is not "naked" as with prokaryotic cells.

10. B: The Biological Species Concept (BSC) states that the status of "species" is based on the natural reproductive isolation of populations. Populations that could potentially interbreed and produce fertile offspring but do not do so in nature are considered different species under the BSC. This species concept does not consider the ability to interbreed under artificial conditions: if two groups do not breed with one another for any reason (in nature), they are reproductively isolated and therefore different species according to the BSC. The isolation may be due to geography, behavior, appearance, or other factors. For example, the Eastern and Western meadowlark look very similar and have overlapping territories, but they have different songs. Individual meadowlarks identify others by their songs and only breed with those with the same song. Because the two populations are reproductively isolated from one another, they are considered different species under the BSC. If individuals with different songs did interbreed and produce fertile offspring, they would be considered the same species.

11. A: The kinetic energy of the gas molecules is directly proportional to the temperature. If the temperature decreases, so does the molecular motion. A decrease in temperature will not necessarily mean a gas condenses to a liquid. Neither the mass nor the density is impacted, as no material was added or removed, and the volume remained the same.

12. C: Vinegar fizzing when poured on a rock is an example of chemical weathering. Mechanical and chemical weathering are processes that break down rocks. Mechanical weathering breaks down rocks physically but does not change their chemical composition. Frost and abrasion are examples. Water, oxygen, carbon dioxide, and living organisms can lead to the chemical weathering of rock. Vinegar is a weak acid and will undergo a chemical reaction, evidenced by fizzing, with the rock. Choice A, rain freezing on the roadway, is an example of the phase change of water from a liquid to a solid and may lead to physical weathering. Choice B, ivy growing on the side of a wooden house, is incorrect since the house is not a rock. Choice D, a river carrying sediment downstream, is an example of erosion.

13. A: The period of a simple pendulum depends on the length and the rate of acceleration due to gravity. The period is independent of amplitude (to a good approximation) for amplitudes less than about 15 degrees. The period of a pendulum is unaffected by increasing the mass.

14. C: As a haploid cell, normal human sperm must contain one chromosome of each of the 23 chromosome pairs. Twenty-two of these pairs are autosomal chromosomes, which do not play a role in determining gender. The remaining pair consists of either two X chromosomes in the case of a female, or of an X and a Y chromosome in the case of a male. Therefore, a normal sperm cell will contain 22 autosomal chromosomes and either an X or a Y chromosome—but not both—for a total of 23.

15. C: In order to have accurate measurements, the use of a graduated cylinder would be best. A triple beam balance measures the mass of an object in grams. A flask and a test tube are used to contain a liquid while being heated or stored.

16. C: The data is relatively consistent with the exception of trial 1. When an experiment is repeated using the same process multiple times, the data from each trial should be very similar or the same. The results of trial 1 indicate that an error may have occurred in the procedure yielding inaccurate results.

17. D: Once a hypothesis has been verified and accepted, it becomes a theory. A theory is a generally accepted explanation that has been highly developed and tested. A theory can explain data and be expected to predict outcomes of tests. A fact is considered to be an objective and verifiable observation, whereas a scientific theory is a greater body of accepted knowledge, principles, or relationships that might explain a fact. A law is an explanation of events for which the outcome is always the same. A conclusion is more of an opinion and could be based on observation, evidence, fact, laws, or even beliefs.

18. B: Animals belonging to the phylum Echinodermata have tube feet for locomotion and feeding. About 7,000 species are extant in this phylum, including starfish and sand dollars. Tube feet are an organ system that provides locomotion, respiration, feeding, and sensory functions. Not all echinoderms have appendages. Having an exoskeleton made of chitin is characteristic of arthropods. Not all echinoderms shed their outer layer of skin to grow.

19. D: Refer to the complete Punnett square in the explanation for question 10. Because male-pattern baldness is recessive, the offspring would need the *bb* gene combination in order to inherit this trait. Therefore, any offspring with the *B* gene will have a full head of hair. Possibilities 1, 2, and 3 all have the *B* gene.

20. A: In a closed system (when you ignore outside interactions), the total momentum is constant and conserved. The total energy would also be conserved, although not the sum of the potential and kinetic energy. Some of the energy from the collision would be turned into thermal energy (heat) for example. Nor is the total velocity conserved, even though the velocity is a component of the momentum, since the momentum also depends on the mass of the cars. The impulse is a force over time that causes the momentum of a body to change. It doesn't make sense to think of impulse as conserved, since it's not necessarily constant throughout a collision.

21. D: When diluting acids, the acid should always be added to the water. This way, if splashing occurs, only water is splashed out of the beaker. Additionally, this procedure ensures that only a small amount of acid is present in a much larger volume of water. This is especially important when diluting sulfuric acid, because large amounts of heat may be released in the hydration process, which could cause a small amount of water to boil rapidly.

22. C: Fossils are least likely to be found in igneous rock. Igneous rock is formed by extreme heat as magma escapes through the Earth's crust and cools. The remains of plants and animals in fossil form are not usually preserved under these conditions. Sedimentary rock (A) is where most fossils are found. Sedimentary rock is formed more slowly and is very abundant. Since soft mud and silts compress into layers, organisms can also be deposited. Metamorphic rock (B) is rock that has undergone change by heat and pressure. This usually destroys any fossils, but occasionally fossil remains are simply distorted and can be found in metamorphic rock.

23. B: Acids and bases will react violently if accidentally mixed, as will reducing and oxidizing agents. Both reactions can be highly exothermic and uncontrollable.

24. C: Repeating the experiment validates data. Each separate experiment is called a repetition. It should be possible to replicate the results of experiments or tests. Similar data gathered from many experiments can also be used to quantify the validity of the hypothesis. Repeating the experiments allows the student to observe variation in the results. Variation in data can be caused by a variety of errors or may be evidence against the hypothesis. Answer D, create a hypothesis, comes before experiments. Answer A, communicate the results, and B, draw a conclusion, occur after testing.

25. A: The structure of the Milky Way galaxy is spiral, meaning it has curved "arms" stretching out from a central point. While spiral galaxies have a flat, disc-like appearance, elliptical galaxies are more three-dimensional and appear to be roughly the same shape regardless of the viewing angle.

26. B: Technology often results from scientific discoveries. The relationship between science and technology is evident when scientific discoveries prompt technologic advances.

27. A: The appearance of the Coriolis effect in the Earth's oceans is caused by the Earth's rotation. The Coriolis effect results when free objects such as water move over a rotating surface such as the Earth. As water moves from the poles towards the equator, it curves slightly westward, while water moving in the opposite direction (from the equator towards the poles) moves slightly eastward.

28. B: Anthers contain microspore mother cells that undergo meiosis to produce microspores. Each microspore then undergoes mitosis to develop into a pollen grain, which is the male gametophyte of flowering plants.

29. A: A ribosome is a structure of eukaryotic cells that makes proteins.

30. B: The process that causes lithospheric plates to move over the surface of the mantle is called convection. The mantle rock in the lower portion of the mantle is heated by the Earth's core and slowly rises to the surface, pushing aside cooler rock that is already there. This hotter rock eventually cools and is pushed aside by hotter rock that rises from below. This cycle, called convection, creates constant movement in the mantle that contributes to the motion of the tectonic plates.

31. D: An inversion mutation is represented in the sequence 1 5 4 3 2 6. An inversion error is a type of mutation where an entire sequence of DNA is reversed. In this case, 2 3 4 5 has been reversed to 5 4 3 2. Answer A, breakage, in a gene can mess up its function entirely or lead to a translocation of genetic information. Answer B, deletion, is when a section of DNA is omitted or lost. Answer C, insertion, is when an extra base pair is added to a DNA sequence. Deletions and insertions can lead to a frameshift effect where entire sequences are thrown off because one nucleotide is wrong. This could result in coding for the wrong amino acid and non-functioning proteins.

32. C: Chloroplasts contain the light-absorbing compound chlorophyll, which is essential in photosynthesis. This gives leaves their green color. Chloroplasts also contain yellow and red carotenoid pigments, which give leaves red and yellow colors in the fall as chloroplasts lose their chlorophyll.

33. C: Either wavelength or frequency can determine the classification of an electromagnetic wave (i.e., radio waves, microwaves, infrared radiation, visible light, ultraviolet radiation, x-rays, gamma rays). The intensity of an electromagnetic wave is independent from its classification. The speed of light is a constant and, as such, is what allows either wavelength or frequency to describe the wave.

34. A: A good hypothesis is testable and logical, and can be used to predict future events. A good hypothesis is also simple, not complex.

35. A: An inch is about $2.54 \text{ cm} = 25.4 \text{ mm} = 2.54 \times 10^{-5} \text{ km} = 2.54 \times 10^{-2} \text{ m}$.

36. A: By comparing the products to the reactants, there must be at least two Al atoms in the starting material, and at least three sulfate groups. Therefore, a coefficient of 2 must be placed in front of $Al(OH)_3$ and a coefficient of 3 must be placed in front of H_2SO_4. To make the number of hydrogen and oxygen atoms equal on both sides of the equation, a coefficient of 6 must be placed in front of H_2O.

37. B: When working with flammable materials or an open flame, the accessible location of the fire blanket and extinguisher must be known in order to maintain safety. However, should the flames not go out immediately or spread too quickly, immediately leave the room and call 911. Close the door behind you in an effort to contain the fire.

38. D: After a secondary consumer dies, such as a wolf, its body is partially consumed by decomposers, such as bacteria and fungi. Bacteria and fungi live in soil and digest body tissues of dead organisms, converting them into basic nutrients that plants need to grow. Therefore, after secondary consumers die, their energy is consumed by decomposers, who make nutrients available in the soil for producers to use. *Do not confuse nutrients in the soil with energy that producers get from the Sun to make their own food.*

39. C: The Sun's energy is the energy source behind Earth's weather patterns, but since the Sun's energy only directly reaches a fraction of Earth's landmass, other factors play an enormous role in distributing the energy globally. The ocean absorbs the Sun's energy and transports it throughout the world, acting as the primary driving force behind global climate and weather. Wind belts, the Earth's orbit, and atmospheric conditions also play a role in driving global weather.

40. B: Bacteria and cyanobacteria have cell walls constructed from peptidoglycans—a polysaccharide and protein molecule. Other types of organisms with cell walls, for instance, plants and fungi, have cell walls composed of different polysaccharides. Plant cell walls are composed of cellulose, and fungal cell walls are composed of chitin.

41. C: An irrigation scheme that draws water from a river and redistributes the water in the local area leads to an increase in evaporation, not a decrease. This is largely due to the increase in the surface area of contact of the water and the atmosphere.

42. C: Plasmids are small circular pieces of DNA found in bacteria. Plasmids are widely used in recombinant DNA technology. They are cut with restriction enzymes and DNA of interest is ligated to them. They can then easily be used to transform bacteria.

43. A: When two tectonic plates are moving laterally in opposing directions, this is called a transform boundary. When there is friction at transform boundaries and pressure builds up, it can result in shallow earthquakes (usually at a depth of less than 25 meters). California's San Andreas Fault is an example of a transform boundary.

44. C: Although there are two cell divisions in meiosis, DNA replication occurs only once. It occurs in interphase I, before M phase begins.

45. A: The rising and falling of the ocean's tides are directly influenced by the gravitational pull of the moon on the earth. High tide is found in areas closest and farthest from the moon because the moon pulls the water and earth toward it, leaving the water on the other side of the earth behind. Low tide occurs in the areas not affected by high tide. There are two tides each day.

46. D: Smallpox is the only disease that has been eradicated by immunization. Progress has been made in the elimination of measles, mumps, and polio.

47. A: When metamorphic rock is stressed unevenly during recrystallization, it can result in foliation. Foliation is characterized by banded rock, and it occurs when certain types of minerals are reoriented during recrystallization due to uneven shortening or compression of the rock.

48. D: The disposal of unused zygotes or embryos, and even the multiple embryos lost through successive unsuccessful implants, is an issue to those who believe life begins at conception. If life begins at conception, then regulations covering experimentation on human beings should be followed.

49. B: Vibration is caused by anything physical moving rapidly back and forth. When an object vibrates, the vibrations disturb the medium surrounding it, which may be solid matter, liquids, or gases like the air. Sound does not cause vibrations in the air (A) but vice versa: vibrations in objects create sound waves. The sound caused by vibration is acoustic energy, and vibratory movements disturb their medium, like the air. These vibrations carry sound waves not only in the air, but also in the ear (C) when they reach it. Whereas sound waves traveling through the air and through the outer and middle ear are acoustic energy, once they reach the inner ear, it converts that acoustic energy into electrical energy that is sent via nerves to the brain (D).

50. A: The lithification process results in the formation of sedimentary rocks. During lithification, existing rock is compacted and liquid is squeezed from its pores. Eventually, the rock is cemented together, resulting in sedimentary rock.

51. C: James Hutton is best known for proposing the theory of uniformitarianism. This geological theory, which is essentially the opposite of catastrophism, suggests that the laws and forces acting on the Earth have remained basically the same since the beginning of geologic time.

52. C: Hund's rule states that electrons must populate empty orbitals of similar energy before pairing up. The Aufbau principle states that electrons must fill lower energy orbitals before filling higher energy orbitals. The Pauli Exclusion Principle states that no two electrons in the same atom can have the same four quantum numbers, and, therefore, two electrons in the same orbital will have opposite spins.

53. B: An iron bar moving inside a coil of wire that contains a current would create an electromagnet. Rapidly spinning and rotating electrons inside an iron bar (A) creates a magnetic field. The movement of electrons through a complete circuit (C) is an electric current. Convection currents within the liquid core of Earth's interior (D) create the Earth's magnetic field.

54. A: Magnetic poles occur in pairs known as magnetic dipoles. Individual atoms can be considered magnetic dipoles due to the spin and rotation of the electrons in the atoms. When the dipoles are aligned, the material is magnetic. Choices B, C, and D are all magnetic materials. Therefore, the magnetic dipoles in these materials are not randomly aligned. Only choice A has randomly aligned dipoles.

55. D: Radiation therapy kills cells by damaging the DNA directly or by producing free radicals that damage the cells. Radiation therapy can kill normal cells. Radiation therapy can be used to cure cancer, prevent cancer from returning, shrink tumors, and reduce pain.

56. B: The electrolysis of water is a chemical change that transforms water into hydrogen and oxygen gases. Synthesis reactions are those that combine reactants to form a product, which is the opposite of what happens when electrolyzing water. Reverse osmosis is a technique often used to purify water by forcing impure water through a semipermeable membrane using a pressure differential.

57. D: In a homogeneous solution, the substance that is dissolved is the solute. A mixture of sugar and water is a homogenous solution in which the sugar is the solute, and the water is the solvent. A mixture of salt and water is a homogeneous solution in which the salt is the solute, and the water is the solvent. A mixture of ash in air is a description of smoke, which is a colloid. A mixture of salt and pepper is a heterogeneous mixture.

58. A: The field of view is the diameter of the circle of light that is seen when one looks into the microscope. As the power of the objective increases, the field of view gets smaller. Therefore, the objective with the greatest field of view is the one with the lowest power.

59. D: Strip mining of coal destroys landscapes, forest, and wildlife habitats. Strip mining also causes dust and noise pollution and may contaminate groundwater. Underground coal mining lowers the water table and changes the flow of groundwater and streams.

60. C: Producers always form the base of an energy pyramid as the first trophic level. Each successive level receives about 10% of the energy from the previous level. In this energy pyramid, the second trophic level receives 10% of 6,000 or 600 kilocalories per square meter per year. The third trophic level receives 10% of 600, or 60 kilocalories per square meter per year.

61. B: Albert Einstein is known for both the special theory of relativity and the general theory of relativity. Thomas Edison was an inventor best known for inventing the light bulb and phonograph.

62. C: All line segments on this graph represent acceleration since change in velocity divided by time equals acceleration. The line with the steepest slope represents the greatest acceleration. The steepest line is V, so option C is the correct answer.

63. C: Limestone is a type of sedimentary rock created through both biological and chemical processes. Clastic (A) sedimentary rock forms from clasts or little bits of rock that are compacted and cemented together. Limestone is not a type of volcanic rock (B). Pegmatite (D) is not a type of sedimentary rock; it is an intrusive igneous rock formed underground from cooling volcanic magma.

64. A: Pioneer species colonize vacant habitats, and the first such species in a habitat demonstrate primary succession. Succession on rock or lava often begins with lichens. Lichens need very little organic material and can erode rock into soil to provide a growth substrate for other organisms.

65. B: Some RNA molecules in extant organisms have enzymatic activity; for example, the formation of peptide bonds on ribosomes is catalyzed by an RNA molecule. This and other information have led scientists to believe that the most likely molecules to first demonstrate enzymatic activity were RNA molecules.

66. B: The loudness of a sound is related to the amplitude of the wave and is measured in decibels (dB). Wave frequency is measured in hertz (Hz). Wavelength is measured in meters (m). Wave velocity is measured in meters per second (m/s).

67. B: Elements and compounds are both pure substances. Elements consist of only one type of atom. Compounds consist of more than one type of atom. Molecules may make up either elements or compounds. Mixtures are two or more substances that are physically combined but not chemically united.

68. D: The colors of the visible spectrum from the lowest to highest frequency are red, orange, yellow, green, blue, and violet. Therefore, violet has the highest frequency.

69. A: Descriptive studies look at and analyze the characteristics of a population or compare aspects across multiple populations. These studies seek information about the state of a population as it is rather than experimentally investigating cause-and-effect relationships by manipulating variables and observing outcomes. Comparing the heights of male and female penguins is an example of a descriptive study. The subject is strictly an observable measure (height) of established populations (male and female). For the other studies, the focus is on the cause-and-effect relationship between a manipulated variable (different media, drug vs. placebo, and old vs. new descriptions) and a result of interest (growth rate, drug efficacy, sales).

70. A: Quartzite, marble, and slate are all examples of metamorphic rocks, while granite is one of the most common types of igneous rocks.

71. A: The higher the temperature of the liquid, the greater the solubility of the solid, while the higher the temperature, the lower the solubility of the gas.

72. B: When scientists and students are able to identify patterns and find meaning in the results of their experiments, they are using the process skill of Inference. When they use the results of their experiments to formulate new hypotheses (A), they are using the process skill of Prediction. When they identify the properties of objects or situations using their senses, they are using the process skill of Observation. When they report the results of their experiments and their conclusions based on these results to others (D), they are using the process skill of Communication. These skills are required for solving both math and science problems.

73. C: Vectors have a magnitude (e.g., 5 meters/second) and direction (e.g., towards north). Of the choices listed, only velocity is defined as a vector. Speed, distance, and time are all quantities that have a size but not a direction. That's why, for example, a car's speedometer reads 35 miles/hour, but does not indicate your direction of travel.

74. D: Accuracy is determined by finding the range of differences between the measured values and the actual value. The smaller the differences, the greater the accuracy. The range of differences for the triple beam balance is between 0.004 and 0.016. The range of differences for the digital balance is between 0.001 and 0.002. Therefore, the digital balance is more accurate. Precision is determined by finding the difference between the highest and lowest readings for each balance. The smaller the difference, the greater the precision. This range for the triple beam balance is 0.02. This range for the digital balance is 0.001. Therefore, the digital balance is also more precise.

75. B: Gradualism states that evolution occurs slowly, with organisms exhibiting small changes over long periods of time. According to gradualism, the fossil record should show gradual changes over time. Punctuated equilibrium states that evolution occurs in spurts of sudden change. According to punctuated equilibrium, the fossil record should have large gaps.

76. D: Benefits to using fossil fuels include that they are cheap and reliable and relatively safe to extract. The technology to control pollution is already developed. The most serious drawback to using fossil fuels is that their pollution contributes greatly to global warming.

77. C: Translation is the process of the tRNA bringing the correct amino acid to the ribosome according to the sequence of the mRNA. Since translation only involves RNA, the four bases are adenine (A), cytosine (C), guanine (G), and uracil (U). There is no thymine (T) used in RNA. Cytosine (C) and guanine (G) pair and adenine (A) and uracil (U) pair. A codon is the triplet sequence that represents a specific amino acid or a start/stop point. It is on the messenger RNA (mRNA). The anticodon is on tRNA and corresponds to the amino acid used by the ribosome during translation.

They are complementary. UGC becomes AUG; AUG becomes CGA. The mRNA codon sequence is U G C A U G C G A if the anticodon sequence formed during translation is A C G U A C G C U.

78. C: Graham's law of diffusion allows one to calculate the relative diffusion rate between two different gases based on their masses.

79. B: Light travels in straight lines. As light moves from one substance to another, the light rays bend according to the refractive index of each substance. As the light travels through the air, it hits the non-submerged portion of the pencil. The light is reflected from the pencil and this is what we see. However, as the light travels *into* the water, the light waves are bent (refracted), and that light is subsequently reflected and travels to our eyes. What we perceive is a pencil that is no longer whole and straight, but broken and bent. It is refraction that causes this perception.

Although the other distractors are also properties of waves, they are not the reasons why the observer perceives the pencil as bent.

80. B: Carbon is released in the form of CO_2 through respiration, burning, and decomposition.

81. A: A scientific theory is a dynamic set of ideas that attempts to explain a scientific phenomenon. Scientific theories are not proven fact. Scientific facts, or laws, are based in extensive evidence and concrete knowledge about our world and are widely accepted descriptions of an aspect of reality. Choice A lists a theory, the Big Bang, which refers to a set of ideas about the origin of the universe. The laws of motion are proven facts that explain the behavior of objects in our environment. Choices B and D both list sets of theories without facts. Choice C shows two scientifically accepted facts, those of mass and electricity conservation and the process of carbon-14 dating of objects.

82. D: Combustion of coal releases significant amounts of Hg into the atmosphere. When the Hg settles into the water, it becomes methylated and concentrates in fish, making them toxic to eat.

83. D: The amount of potential energy an object has depends on mass, height above ground and gravitational attraction, but not temperature. The formula for potential energy is $PE = mgh$, or potential energy equals mass times gravity times height. Answers (A), (B), and (C) are all valid answers as they are all contained in the formula for potential energy. Potential energy is the amount of energy stored in a system particularly because of its position.

84. B: Water that evaporates from oceans can precipitate over land due to advection. Advection is the horizontal movement of air masses by wind. Moist air over the ocean is transported horizontally over land; as this air rises and cools (often by convection or lifting over terrain or fronts), the water vapor condenses and can precipitate over land masses.

85. B: When the accumulation of snow and ice exceeds ablation, a glacier will gradually form. Ablation is the sloughing off of ice and snow through melting, evaporation, sublimation, and wind erosion. When snow and ice accumulate faster than ablation occurs, a glacier will form and continue to gain mass until the rate of ablation overtakes the rate of accumulation.

86. D: Endocytosis is a process by which cells absorb larger molecules or even tiny organisms, such as bacteria, that would not be able to pass through the plasma membrane. Endocytic vesicles containing molecules from the extracellular environment often undergo further processing once they enter the cell.

87. B: Photosynthesis converts carbon dioxide into sugars that plants use. Three types of photosynthesis are C3, C4, and CAM. C3 is used by most plants. C4 plants live in areas with high temperatures and high light exposure. C4 first forms a four-carbon sugar instead of the three-carbon sugar formed by C3. Also, the stomata of C4 plants are faster at absorbing carbon dioxide and do not have to open as long, so less water is lost by transpiration. A C4 plant, such as saltbush, corn, or some grasses, would live in a very hot environment rather than a cold, marine, or dark environment. Plants that use the CAM (Crassulacean Acid Metabolism) type of photosynthesis also use water more efficiently as their stomata are closed during the day and open at night. Desert cacti are examples.

88. A: The human body works best within a certain temperature range, around 98.6°F. When the body gets too cold or too hot it cannot function properly. The boy who is outside in the winter is cold. His body temperature is dropping below 98.6°F. His muscles start to contract causing him to shiver in order to generate heat. The girl is outside in the summer, and begins sweating to reduce her body temperature from rising too far above 98.6°F. In both cases, the children's bodies are trying to keep the temperature close to 98.6°F.

89. C: Goggles, lab aprons, and gloves are personal protective equipment for an individual to wear as protection against splashing solutions onto clothing or skin or into the eyes and should be worn while working with any chemicals or flammable materials.

90. B: It is true that the asthenosphere is hotter and more fluid than the lithosphere. The asthenosphere is a hot, ductile layer within the upper mantle upon which the lithosphere, or the uppermost mantle and Earth's crust, is situated. Heat is transferred within the asthenosphere through a process called convection, which sometimes causes movement in the tectonic plates that make up the lithosphere.

91. B: When sulfur dioxide and nitrogen dioxide mix with water and other substances in the atmosphere, they produce sulfuric acid and nitric acid. These acids kill plants and animals when they reach the surface of the earth.

92. B: Pros of solar energy include the facts that it is renewable, abundant, environmentally friendly, low maintenance, and silent. Cons of solar energy include that it is expensive and intermittent and requires a lot of space. Solar panels require rare minerals like indium and tellurium and at this point are only about 20% efficient in harvesting energy—putting them behind several other alternative methods. Other solar harvesting methods besides the photoelectric effect include concentrated solar and water heating.

93. D: The formation of sedimentary rock does not include heat. Of the three types of rock—igneous, sedimentary, and metamorphic—heat is essential to two: igneous and metamorphic. Sedimentary rocks are formed by sediments that get deposited and then compacted or cemented together. Sedimentary rocks are classified into detrital, organic, or chemical sediments. Answer A, layering, is correct since sediments can be deposited or otherwise formed in layers. Answer B, cementation, is also called lithification. Answer C, compaction, refers to the pressure forming sedimentary rock leading to cementation.

94. B: Although like charges do repel, and unlike charges do attract, the question is indirectly asking about the law of conservation of charge. In other words, when someone mentions electric charge being conserved, they are saying the net charge of system remains constant. Charge originates from electrons and protons is only partially true because there are other elementary particles with charge. Charge can be created or destroyed because a photon will produce an electron-positron pair. There is also the example of a proton and electron combining to form a neutron.

95. D: The physical structure of the universe is thought to consist of filaments (walls of superclusters, clusters, and galaxies) that surround large, bubble-like voids. Filaments are the largest structures in the universe, with some forming huge structures like the Great Wall and the Sloan Great Wall.

96. A: A formalized hypothesis written in the form of an if/then statement can then be tested. A statement may make a prediction or imply a cause/effect relationship, but that does not necessarily make it a good hypothesis. In this example, the student could rewrite the statement in the form of an if/then statement such as, "If the length of the string of the pendulum is varied, then the time it takes the ball to make one complete period changes." This hypothesis is testable, and doesn't simply make a prediction or a conclusion. The validity of the hypothesis can then be supported or disproved by experimentation and observation.

97. B: Earth's atmosphere is made up of about 78% nitrogen, 21% oxygen, and 1% other gases (including water vapor), making choice B correct. The abundant nitrogen in Earth's atmosphere is left over from the time billions of years ago when volcanoes hurled it into the air. Nitrogen tends to be unreactive and does not readily bond with other elements. Oxygen and hydrogen bond together to make the water that covers much of our planet's surface.

98. B: Phyletic gradualism is the view that evolution occurs at a more or less constant rate. Contrary to this view, punctuated equilibrium holds that evolutionary history consists of long periods of stasis punctuated by geologically short periods of evolution. This theory predicts that there will be few fossils revealing intermediate stages of evolution, whereas phyletic gradualism views the lack of intermediate-stage fossils as a deficit in the fossil record that will resolve when enough specimens are collected.

99. D: The cinder cone volcano is the most common type of volcano on Earth. A cinder cone has steep sides made of fallen cinders, which themselves are made of the lava that intermittently shoots into the air. A composite volcano, sometimes called the stratovolcano, has steep sides, so the explosions of ash, pumice, and silica are often accompanied by treacherous mudslides. Indeed, it is these mudslides that cause most of the damage associated with composite volcano eruptions. Krakatoa and Mount Saint Helens are examples of composite volcanoes. A lava dome is a round volcano that emits thick lava very slowly. A shield volcano, one example of which is Mt. Kilauea in Hawaii, emits a small amount of lava over an extended period of time. Shield volcanoes are not known for violent eruptions.

100. B: Recycling and using alternative sources of energy reduce the amount of pollutants introduced into the ecosystem, reduce the potential for disease-related human maladies, and reduce the reliance on nonrenewable resources. Greater production of goods and consumer spending in the future would probably be good for the economy, but not necessarily the environment. Fossil fuels are considered to be a nonrenewable energy resource.